Scott Stangle

LEAVE NO
TRACE

LEAVE NO TRACE

A Practical Guide to the New Wilderness Ethic

by Annette McGivney

THE
MOUNTAINEERS

THE MAGAZINE OF WILDERNESS TRAVEL

Published by
The Mountaineers
1001 SW Klickitat Way, Suite 201
Seattle, WA 98134

© 1998 by *BACKPACKER* magazine
33 East Minor Street
Emmaus, PA 18098

First printing 1998, second printing 1998, third printing 1999, fourth printing 2001

Published simultaneously in Great Britain by Cordee, 3a DeMontfort Street, Leicester, England, LE1 7HD

Manufactured in the United States of America

Editor: Uma Kukathas
Copyeditor: Kris Fulsaas
BACKPACKER Project Editor: Dorcas Miller
Illustrator: Dawn Peterson
Cover design: Helen Cherullo
Layout: Michelle Taverniti

Cover photograph: *Backpacker watching sunset sky* © Galen Rowell/Corbis
Frontispiece: Four hikers descending a small creek in morning light into N.F. Boulder Creek (photo © Deborah Sussex, courtesy of NOLS)

Library of Congress Cataloging-in-Publication Data
McGivney, Annette.
    Leave no trace : a guide to the new wilderness ethic / by Annette McGiveny. — 1st ed.
        p.   cm.
    Includes bibliographical references (p.   ) and index.
    ISBN 0-89886-524-7
    1. Outdoor recreation—Environmental aspects—United States.
2. Low-impact camping—United States. I. Title.
GV191.4.M35 1998
796.54—dc21   97-46839
                                                           CIP

♻ Printed on recycled paper

Contents

Preface

Imagine you have a house guest, and he does not see anywhere to hang his coat in your living room. So he pulls a hammer and a 4-inch nail out of his pocket and proceeds to drive it into your oak paneling to create his own makeshift coat rack. Then, during dinner, your guest lets his food scraps fall onto the carpet instead of putting them in the trash. And to top off the evening, this recipient of your hospitality, while relieving himself in your bathroom, carelessly tosses used toilet paper on the floor instead of flushing it down the commode.

Such barbaric behavior sounds appalling, even unimaginable, in today's well-mannered society. You are probably thinking you do not know anyone who would come close to acting this way, and that you would have to go back to the Middle Ages to find so-called "civilized" adults tossing trash around in living areas and letting the nasties associated with bodily wastes fall where they may. But if you consider our nation's wilderness areas to be places as special and as deserving of respect as a human home, then you probably know plenty of people who have behaved this way at one time or another—maybe you have even done so yourself.

Wilderness, in most places in the Lower 48 states, does not harbor human houses, but it is home to many other creatures that deserve, at the very least, to live in an unpolluted environment. And for many of us humans—who over the last century have largely become urban animals—the wilderness is one of our favorite places to visit. Spending time in a natural environment, breathing clean air, drinking in wide-open spaces, witnessing the complex beauty of nature's handiwork, is a joyous and much-needed experience for millions of Americans each year. And, considering how quickly urban development has spread in recent decades, and how little of the United States has been set aside as "forever protected" from development under the federal Wilderness

Act of 1964, these precious few wild places are truly a privilege to visit and hardly the location for humans to trash.

Yet, as recently as twenty-five years ago, it was common practice among upstanding American citizens going outdoors to wreak havoc on the environment. Without thinking twice, people would set up camp in pristine areas and nail pegs into trees to hang their lanterns and gear, leave their trash in fire rings and makeshift garbage dumps, and encircle the area with human waste and the telltale "toilet paper flowers." Outdoor youth groups perfected the art of camp craft by descending on an area en masse and going about digging latrines, constructing elaborate fire rings, chopping down trees for firewood and benches, cutting tree boughs for sleeping mats, and digging trenches around tents.

Thanks to a heightened environmental consciousness that has blossomed over the last two decades, most outdoor enthusiasts are now much more aware of their impacts on the land and do not engage in the destructive "camp craft" practices from the days of yore. But beyond cleaning up your trash and not cutting down trees for firewood, how far should you go to minimize your impact? What is really important, from an environmental standpoint, and what is too extreme? Many environmentally conscious, recreation-minded people are not sure.

The purpose of this book is to answer those questions—to introduce you to the principles of Leave No Trace, or the "new wilderness etiquette," and to offer you a guide to very realistic and doable LNT practices and techniques that can be applied to all manner of outdoor pursuits.

To put it simply, Leave No Trace is the practice of traveling and camping with care when visiting wildlands. It requires that we deliberately plan and guide our outdoor experiences so that we do not harm the environment or disturb others.

Leave No Trace is about helping people make better environmental decisions when enjoying the great outdoors. It is not, literally, aimed at ridding wildlands of all signs of human visitation. Unless people were barred from these areas completely, such an objective would be impossible. The philosophy behind teaching people the Leave No Trace ethic—as developed by the National Outdoor Leadership School

(NOLS) and espoused by Leave No Trace, Inc., and all federal land management agencies—supports the notion that humans belong in the wilderness; we just need to make our passing as undetectable as possible. (Founded in 1965 and based in Lander, Wyoming, NOLS is a wilderness-based, nonprofit school focusing on teaching leadership and outdoor skills.)

Attaining a balance between our desire to visit wildlands and doing what it takes to protect these sensitive places from too many visitors is a difficult and often conflicting goal. Land managers call it "limits of acceptable change"; Leave No Trace brochures describe it as "minimizing impact." Either way, this so-called new wilderness etiquette is a very noble and necessary notion, considering the growing human pressures on our public lands. It is the only way we will still be able to enjoy wilderness experiences without destroying the wilderness in the process.

As for how far you want to go in adopting and practicing Leave No Trace techniques, it is strictly up to you and what you are comfortable with (you do not have to pack out human waste and drink your dishwater to be environmentally responsible). There are no LNT police out there enforcing a set of rules, and motivation for abiding by this outdoor ethic should not come from guilt but a desire to respect and enjoy our limited wildlands. Traveling cleanly and quietly through the backcountry—leaving the land as you found it—is not only good for the environment but can be personally satisfying and lead to a heightened wilderness experience.

One final note about this book: the terms "wilderness," "backcountry," and "wildlands" are used synonymously throughout the text. Generally, all three terms are used to refer to public lands that are away from cities and are largely undeveloped. "Wilderness," however, specifically applies to land that is federally designated under the Wilderness Act of 1964. "Backcountry" and "wildlands" are more general terms that encompass not only wilderness areas, but all public lands that are mostly roadless and in a primitive condition.

Leave No Trace practices were originally aimed at protecting wilderness areas and educating backpackers and horse packers visiting those places. However, the minimum-impact approach is now being used to preserve the environmental integrity of all public lands, regardless of whether the land is formally protected under the Wilderness Act. And, consequently, the Leave No Trace message—and this book—is aimed at all outdoor recreationists, from backpackers to mountain bikers to paddlers. I figure we could all benefit from a little schooling in wilderness etiquette to help us be better house guests in the great outdoors.

Grafitti in Sycamore Canyon Wilderness Area, AZ (photo by Mike Frick)

Acknowledgments

Special thanks to David Cole of the U.S. Forest Service Aldo Leopold Research Institute and Jeff Marion of the National Park Service Cooperative Park Studies Unit at Viriginia Polytechnic Institute and State University. Their generous help in offering advice and supplying information was invaluable, and it is upon their extensive research that the principles of the Leave No Trace program are based.

Also, heartfelt gratitude goes to Rich Brame and Marit Sawyer at the NOLS Leave No Trace office, and to Dana Watts at Leave No Trace, Inc. Without their help this book would not have been possible.

Introduction

America's Legacy of Wilderness and the Evolution of the Leave No Trace Ethic

Daniel Webster could not have been more misguided when in 1861 he shared his doubts about the United States' continued push to fulfill its goal of Manifest Destiny and grow the country all the way to the Pacific Ocean. As retold in the book *Westward in Eden*, "What do we want of that vast and worthless area, that region of savages and wild beasts, of wind, of dust, of cactus and prairie dogs?" asked Webster of his fellow congressmen regarding the government's continued acquisition of western lands. "To what use could we ever hope to put those great deserts and those endless mountain ranges, impenetrable and covered to their base in eternal snow?"

Obviously, America's attitude toward its "untamed" public lands has changed dramatically over the last 150 years. Pristine and rugged wilderness areas that were once considered worthless by prominent citizens like Daniel Webster are now cherished places that are guarded by the strictest of environmental laws. Unfortunately, the progression of the United States from a poor, young nation to a world superpower has involved the development of billions of acres of pristine wildlands. And now that the prevailing consensus among U.S. citizens is that our society needs wildlands, there is little true wilderness left to protect.

The current conservation ethic was preceded by an ethic of consumption that emphasized using natural resources purely for economic gain. During most of the nineteenth century, U.S. public lands were valued, not for recreation, but for what could be extracted from them: gold, minerals, timber, rangeland, and an endless supply of acreage for homesteading.

As the National Outdoor Leadership School points out in its Leave

No Trace training manuals in the Skills and Ethics series: "The evolution of a land ethic and appreciation of wildlands are luxuries we in the United States and people throughout much of developed western countries can now afford. Ironically, successful exploitation of natural resources in the United States has placed us in the enviable position of being able to afford the luxury of conservation."

PUBLIC LANDS PRIMER

Within the span of a century, the federally owned "public domain" shrunk from over a billion acres to some 730 million acres, or 32 percent of the total U.S. land area. What is left of our nation's federally owned lands is largely in Alaska and the western Lower 48 states, and most of it falls under the jurisdiction of four federal agencies: the U.S. Forest Service, the National Park Service, the U.S. Fish and Wildlife Service, and the Bureau of Land Management (BLM).

While each agency is managed to fulfill different mandates, all are charged with the dual responsibility of protecting our nation's natural resources and meeting the public's steadily growing desire to recreate on federal lands. And it is to this end that all four agencies have joined together in adopting and promoting the Leave No Trace ethic.

Although only a small percentage of federally owned lands are found east of the Mississippi, the eastern half of the United States nonetheless claims an abundance of recreational areas in the form of state-owned parks, preserves, forests, and game lands, as well as private preserves. In upstate New York, for example, Adirondack Park encompasses 2.5 million acres of public lands, with 2,000 miles of trails; Baxter State Park in Maine has 202,064 acres of wildlands with 175 miles of trails. Much of the 2,100-mile Appalachian Trail, which extends from Maine to Georgia, goes through state lands and privately owned right-of-way.

Although these public lands in the East are generally not as large as the vast expanses of western backcountry, they often have extensive trail networks and campgrounds, and suffer from the same risks of being loved to death as federally owned wildlands. Most of the state lands are managed by separate recreation-oriented agencies—like the New York State Department of Environmental Conservation—which

Fragile Sonoran Desert environment, McDowell Mountain Preserve, AZ (photo by Mike Frick)

include staffs of rangers, biologists, and others similar to those of the federal land management agencies. And, like the federal land management agencies, many of these state-run land management departments are also actively involved in promoting the Leave No Trace program and teaching visitors about minimum-impact techniques.

How did we, as a nation, evolve from a wilderness-loathing mentality like Daniel Webster's to the current state of affairs where government agencies are promoting the Leave No Trace ethic? The evolution of the conservation ethic and America's growing affinity for outdoor recreation really began to take shape with the landmark passage of the Wilderness Act in 1964.

A RETURN TO THE WILDERNESS

In an attempt to protect America's last vestiges of wildlands, and after years of debate, Congress finally passed the sweeping measure in 1964 that established the Wilderness Preservation System. When the Wilderness Act was approved, 9.1 million acres of federal lands were automatically incorporated into the system. Today, designated wilderness totals some 103 million acres and is found on lands managed by the Forest Service, Park Service, Fish and Wildlife Service, and BLM.

These wilderness preserves, as defined by the law, are "areas where the earth and its community of life are untrammeled by man, where man himself is a visitor who does not remain." The respective land management agency in charge of the land on which the designated areas are located is responsible for fulfilling the mandate of the Wilderness Act and keeping the preserves "untrammeled." Consequently, motorized vehicles and mountain bikes are banned from all federal wilderness areas. The construction of roads and any kind of commercial development is also not allowed. And unless it was "grandfathered" in to the enabling legislation when a specific wilderness area was designated by Congress, consumptive uses like grazing, mining, logging, and oil extraction are also off-limits in these most highly protected lands. The only way to travel through a wilderness area is self-propelled—by foot, horseback, or paddle.

After the Wilderness Act was passed, the various federal land management agencies conducted inventories of their holdings and identified all roadless areas larger than 5,000 acres that they felt were suitable for wilderness designation. In most states, the wilderness designation process has been completed and Congress has passed state wilderness bills that supposedly set aside our nation's major roadless areas for preservation. Although obtaining wilderness status for the 103 million acres of federal land currently part of the Wilderness Preservation System is an environmental victory, the battle for preservation of wildlands is far from over.

One need only leaf through *The Big Outside: A Descriptive Inventory of the Big Wilderness Areas of the United States,* by Dave Foreman and Howie Wolke, to get a feel for all the worthy wildlands that have not been designated as wilderness and given the protection they deserve. Even though the opening paragraph of the Wilderness Act clearly states that "it is the policy of Congress to secure for the American people of present and future generations the benefits of an enduring resource of wilderness," when it comes to politics, short-term gains almost always win over lofty, long-term goals. In western states, where most of the eligible, large roadless areas are located, large chunks of federal lands that conservationists say should be a shoo-in for wilderness designation have been passed over because of vocal objections from consumptive users of the land like logging and mining companies.

In Arizona, for example, the Forest Service identified 2.1 million acres as potentially suitable for wilderness designation, and conservation groups argued that all of the land should be protected under the Wilderness Preservation System. But, in the end, only 767,000 acres were federally designated as part of the 1984 Arizona Wilderness Act, and the largest stands of old-growth ponderosa pine forest in the Southwest were left open to logging. Elsewhere in the West, wars over wilderness designation still rage in Utah—where conservationists are pushing for 5.7 million acres to be protected, but the state's congressional delegation wants less than half that amount—and in Colorado, Idaho, and Alaska.

Meanwhile, federal land managers are struggling in many designated wilderness areas to keep the land in an "untrammeled" condition. As David Cole of the U.S. Forest Service's Aldo Leopold Research

Signs of impact begin to show in a camp area. (photo courtesy of NOLS)

Institute observed in a report titled *Wilderness Recreation Use Trends,* "Recreation use of the National Wilderness Preservation System increased almost sixfold between 1965 and 1994 when recreation use approached 17 million visitor days." (A visitor day is defined as one person visiting the area for 12 hours.) Cole added that, "In 1994 [the most recent data he had available], recreation use intensity, excluding Alaska, was as high as it has ever been—about 0.4 recreation visitor days per acre."

Cole has also observed that, compared to their backpacking brethren of the 1960s, wilderness travelers of the 1990s seem to be more hurried and have less of a purist attitude about their experience. "Today's visitors are more likely to support high-standard (developed) trails, bridges over small creeks, and administrative use of chain saws to clear trails," noted Cole in an article titled "The Changing Wilderness." "They are less likely to support low-standard trails and leaving a few trees blown down across the trail. In other words, they appear to be more interested in comfortable and convenient access than before."

While backpacking and horse packing in wilderness areas continue to have a steady, if not slightly increased, participation rate, it is the day hiker who seems to be headed to these preserves in droves. Day hiking is, by far, the fastest-growing activity in wilderness areas. And, not surprisingly, wildlands that are located within a few hours' drive of metropolitan areas are being most heavily impacted by increased visitation.

LEAVE NO TRACE IS BORN

Dealing with increasing visitation and resulting environmental impacts is part and parcel of being a land manager today, but few managers were prepared thirty years ago for the recreation boom that happened after the Wilderness Act was passed. A public survey conducted by Edward Spencer and others in 1965 for the Bureau of Outdoor Recreation showed that 9.9 million Americans hiked or backpacked. This figure increased to more than 28 million when the survey was repeated in 1977.

The problem back then was not only with the number of people descending upon wilderness areas, but with the high-impact approach

High-tech equipment such as waterproof rain gear has made it possible for more people to enjoy wilderness travel. (photo courtesy of NOLS)

most people took (albeit unknowingly) when visiting the great out-doors. Millions of people visiting the backcountry and practicing camp-ing techniques from a bygone era caused wildlands in many places to look more like the back alleys of third-world villages rather than land that had been set aside for the express purpose of protection from de-velopment.

Alpine lakes became polluted from human waste; trails eroded to levels that were sometimes knee-deep; campsites became devoid of vegetation and were often host to growing mounds of discarded refuse, including everything from tin cans to broken backpacks. It all added up to a big dilemma for land managers, who are charged with the dual responsibilities of environmental protection of the resource and ac-commodation of people's desire to recreate on public lands.

"In the 1970s, it was socially acceptable to have fire rings and litter everywhere at wilderness campsites," recalled Tom Alt, a forestry technician with the Beartooth District of the Custer National Forest in Montana and Wyoming, in a recent conversation. In fact, land managers in the Beartooth-Absaroka Wilderness during that time found themselves packing out "mule-trains" of trash left behind by careless campers.

To get a handle on overuse and abuse of America's wilderness areas, land managers had two primary options—they could close damaged areas to the public or, as Alt explained, they could try to educate wilderness users in more environmentally sound camping techniques, to "show people a better way." The educational program that Alt and his Forest Service colleagues developed sixteen years ago came to be called "No Trace." Meanwhile, the Forest Service in Utah had developed a similar program called "Leave No Trace" to deal with visitor impacts in the Uinta Mountains.

"When [No Trace] first got started, we had to teach people the basics—that you did not leave garbage piles, that you did not tie horses to trees, and that you did not need to have large campfires," said Alt. "People generally knew littering was wrong, but they were not aware of the impact of human waste in the wilderness, and how long it takes toilet paper to decompose." Alt's district, along with other National Forest districts across the country, also began implementing policies dictating how far camps should be set back from the water, campfire restrictions, and visitor permit systems. "People have generally been very receptive to the low-impact message, but, for some, old ways die hard," he said.

Nevertheless, Alt's education program has had a big impact, reaching some 41,000 people in Montana, including many school-aged children and outdoor groups. Well-meaning visitors are no longer leaving trash piles, cutting tree boughs, or trenching around tents in the Beartooth Wilderness. "I say this with trepidation, but things have gotten better," noted Alt. "We have more visitors now than in the '70s, but the impacts are less."

THE LNT GOSPEL SPREADS

The success of Alt's program in the Beartooths gradually encouraged other land managers across the country to embrace the concept of a public education program to teach people techniques in minimum-impact camping and wilderness travel. While closure of overused areas, visitor quota systems, and the implementation of designated

Participants in an LNT Masters course learn about fire rings and campsite impacts. (photo courtesy of NOLS)

campsites have been important management tools over the last few decades in keeping our precious wildlands from being loved to death, visitor education is by far the most socially palatable and often the most effective solution.

By the early 1980s, there were numerous minimum-impact education programs circulating through the federal land management agencies. Slogans like "pack it in; pack it out," "tread lightly," "take only pictures, leave only footprints," and "give a hoot, don't pollute" became familiar to backcountry visitors. And just about everyone got the message that litter was a big no-no, that human fecal matter required a proper burial, and that toilet paper was not to be treated as some kind of groundcover. However, beyond these basic dos and don'ts, the low-impact mantra varied greatly with each program, each land management agency, and almost every district office. The lack of a uniform message led to confusion among wilderness users and, in many cases, made the land manager's dual job of recreation enabler and environmental steward that much more difficult.

Enter Bill Thompson, a thirty-four-year U.S. Forest Service veteran who has worked in Forest Service districts throughout the West. In 1990, the Forest Service asked Thompson if he would take on the job as the agency's first Leave No Trace coordinator, and promote the minimum-impact concept as a national program. By 1993 a "memorandum of understanding" was signed between the four federal land management agencies (U.S. Forest Service, National Park Service, Bureau of Land Management, and U.S. Fish and Wildlife Service) and the nonprofit National Outdoor Leadership School (NOLS), which established Leave No Trace as the nation's official wilderness ethics program.

Thompson had enlisted NOLS, based in Lander, Wyoming, to spearhead the education component of the program. NOLS collaborated with the BLM, Forest Service, National Park Service, and recreation ecologists Jeff Marion and David Cole to develop the six basic principles of the Leave No Trace program and a standard LNT curriculum. That curriculum is now taught to land managers, youth group leaders, outdoor organizations, and others who disseminate a cohesive, consistent message to wildland users. NOLS staff members Drew Leemon, Susan Chadwick Brame, and John Gookin drew from information on minimum-impact research and techniques they had developed for NOLS instructors to create LNT materials that could be mass-marketed across the country. Brochures, pamphlets, videos, and information cards describing LNT skills and ethics for different environments have since been developed by NOLS, with the aid and input of numerous land managers, outfitters, and recreation groups. Learning kits and teaching tools have also been produced to educate children, as well as adults, about LNT techniques.

In 1994, a new nonprofit organization was created to further expand the scope and reach of the Leave No Trace program. Based in Boulder, Colorado, Leave No Trace, Inc., is charged with coordinating all national LNT partnership, licensing, and fund-raising efforts. The organization unites the four federal land management agencies with manufacturers and retailers of outdoor gear, user groups, and educators who are involved in spreading the LNT message. LNT materials are distributed by Leave No Trace, Inc., LNT partners, and land management offices across the country. A toll-free number is available for folks seeking information and materials on LNT practices (see the appendix).

"My personal feeling all along has been that education—teaching people a new wilderness ethic—is the only way," said Thompson in a recent conversation. "Closing areas was not a good option."

PRINCIPLES TO LIVE BY

When teaching LNT skills and ethics, NOLS stresses that the six basic principles around which the minimum-impact ethic has been built are not hard-and-fast rules, but guidelines aimed at helping backcountry users make ecologically sound decisions in various environments and situations. These guidelines are the foundation of what has become a new wilderness etiquette, an ethic toward recreating in the backcountry that is eons from the days when it was common practice to turn campsites into garbage dumps. Throughout this book, the principles of Leave No Trace are expanded upon, but here is the encapsulated version of six guidelines to live by when visiting the great outdoors:

Plan Ahead and Prepare
- Call ahead to the place you intend to visit to find out about any special environmental concerns, regulations, or permits.
- Be prepared for harsh conditions by bringing proper equipment and knowing how to use it.
- Carefully plan meals so that there is no food waste. Reduce your amount of trash by repackaging food in reusable containers.
- Invest in modern gear that aids in environmentally responsible camping. Use a lightweight stove to replace the need for cooking over fires; get a tent with a watertight floor; become the proud owner of a trowel to aid in the digging of cat holes.
- Try to stay away from popular areas during times of high use, such as holidays and weekends. If you are in a group of four or more, take special care to avoid popular areas during busy times.

Camp and Travel on Durable Surfaces
- Help mitigate trampling and erosion problems by staying on designated trails; walk in single file in the middle of the path.
- When traveling cross-country where there are no trails, try to stay on the most durable surfaces—rock, gravel, dry grasses, or snow.

Hike on established trails whenever possible. (photo by Mike Frick)

- In areas frequented by visitors, camp at a designated site that shows obvious signs of use—soil is compacted, vegetation is sparse. And keep your activities concentrated in the impacted area.
- If you are lucky enough to be in a pristine area that shows few signs of human visitation, disperse your individual impact by camping in a never-before-used site. Stay away from campsites that have already been lightly impacted.

Pack It In; Pack It Out
- Do not be a slob—be careful not to disrupt wildlife by leaving food scraps around camp.

- Keep your gear organized in camp so that you do not accidentally leave something behind.
- Burying trash is not a good idea, because wildlife will just dig it up, and burning it is not environmentally sound either.

Properly Dispose of What You Cannot Pack Out

- You can pack out your poop if you really want to, but it is perfectly acceptable in most wilderness areas to bury it in a cat hole that is 4 to 8 inches deep and at least 200 feet from water, camp, or trails.
- Scrutinize your need for toilet paper; nature provides a variety of environmentally friendly tissue alternatives. If you must use toilet paper, pack it out.
- Keep pollutants out of water sources by camping at least 200 feet from lakes and streams.
- To wash yourself or your dishes, carry water 200 feet from streams or lakes, and use small amounts of biodegradable soap. Strain dishwater with a cloth and then scatter the water or sump.

Leave What You Find

- For starters, it is against federal law to disturb archaeological or historic sites. Do not disturb these relics of our nation's heritage, and camp well away from such sites.
- Observe wildlife from a distance and do not feed the animals.
- Avoid altering a campsite—such as driving a nail in a tree or making a bench out of a log—to accommodate your desires for comfort. If you move a log or rock to improve a sleeping area, replace it when leaving camp.
- Take home memories instead of souvenirs such as interesting rocks or wildflowers.

Minimize Use and Impact of Fires

- Although a cozy and longtime tradition, campfires can cause permanent scars to an area; use a stove instead.
- If you must have a fire, use an existing fire ring or build a no-trace mound or pan fire.

- For fuel, gather sticks from the ground that are no larger in diameter than an adult's wrist. Do not pull branches off dead or downed trees.
- When vacating the site, put out your fire completely, pack out all unburned trash from the fire ring, and scatter the cool ashes over a large area well away from camp.

These basic principles are just the beginning to establishing a new wilderness etiquette. David Cole, a recreation ecologist for the U.S. Forest Service's Intermountain Research Station, has conducted a number of studies on visitor impact to wilderness areas. In a telephone conversation, he pointed out, "Levels of trash may be better today, but the land is still being significantly affected by growing numbers of people."

The success of the Forest Service, BLM, National Park Service, and U.S. Fish and Wildlife Service in communicating the basic Leave No Trace message over the last decade has been tempered by the ever-increasing demand for recreation on public lands. Even if most people are picking up their litter, the sheer volume of visitors has led to a host of environmental and aesthetic problems in the backcountry—like vegetation loss from trampling and decreased opportunities for solitude. The need for protecting visitor solitude, along with the environmental resource, is what has compelled Cole to add a seventh LNT principle to articles and research papers he has written on the subject of low-impact recreation. "Minimize noise and visual intrusion," he urges. "Solitude can be maximized by doing everything reasonable to stay hidden from other users."

So while the Leave No Trace concept can be boiled down into a few basic guidelines, it actually goes far beyond convincing people to pack out what they pack in. It is about gaining an understanding of the environment and knowing how to enjoy America's precious wildlands without harming them. And it is about having respect for fellow recreationists and their desires to enjoy the land. Protecting the backcountry through wilderness designations and land management regulations is not enough. Ultimately, preservation of our nation's wildlands comes down to visitor attitudes and our willingness to practice this new wilderness etiquette.

▲ ▲ ▲

How the West Was Lost and Won
A History of the U.S. Frontier and Federal Land Management

Beginning with the Louisiana Purchase in 1803, in which the United States doubled its geographic size with the stroke of a pen, the vast wilderness between the Mississippi River and the Pacific Ocean became American territory. Treaties and purchases between the U.S. government and Spain, Great Britain, Mexico, and the Republic of Texas grew our nation from sea to shining sea in just fifty years. Plus, the acquisition of Alaska from Russia in 1867 added another 365 million acres to the U.S. land base.

While the United States was acquiring some of the most scenic and ecologically diverse wilderness on the planet, the federal government's plan was not to preserve it for posterity but, rather, to use the land to grow the nation's economy. In 1812, the General Land Office was established to "dispose" of federally owned lands—called the "public domain"—and put the abundant natural resources in the hands of private individuals and enterprises for development. Because much of the land in the East and the Midwest had already passed into private ownership by then, most of the public domain that was up for grabs was in the West—the rugged Rockies, the grasslands of the Great Plains, the canyons of the Southwest, and the towering redwood forests of the Pacific Coast.

Although the idea of wholesale development of these pristine lands for the sake of commerce may make modern-day conservationists cringe, few questioned the motives or methods for profiting from western wilderness in the nineteenth century. In fact, as William K. Wayant points out in *WESTWARD IN EDEN*, it was cause for great excitement and hype among many business-minded people, like Thaddeus Mason Harris of Massachusetts. In *WESTWARD IN EDEN*, we find

Harris's account of the pioneer settlements he saw on his journey down the Ohio River through the Northwest Territory in 1803:

When we see the land cleared of those enormous trees with which it was overgrown, and the cliffs and quarries converted into materials for building, we cannot help dwelling upon the industry and art of man, which by dint of toil and perseverance can change the desert into a fruitful field, and shape the rough rock to use...When the solitary waste is peopled, and convenient habitations arise amidst the former retreats of wild beasts; when the silence of nature is succeeded by the buzz of employment...when we behold competence and plenty springing from the bosom of dreary forests—what a lesson is afforded of the benevolent intentions of Providence!

The Homestead Act of 1862 was the most benevolent in a series of federal laws that encouraged unrestricted settlement of the West in an attempt to fulfill such "providence." Under the measure, any hearty soul could claim 160 acres of public domain as his private property just by living on it for five years. It was an enticing offer for millions of people residing east of the Mississippi, as well as European immigrants fresh off the boat from land-scarce countries. But as Roderick Nash points out in his book *WILDERNESS AND THE AMERICAN MIND*, homesteading rugged Western lands was no panacea; consequently, the wilderness was viewed by frontier settlers as Public Enemy Number One—right up there with the devil.

"Two components figured in the American pioneer's bias against wilderness," wrote Nash. "On the direct, physical level, it constituted a formidable threat to his very survival. Safety and comfort, even necessities like food and shelter, depended on overcoming the wild environment. In addition,

civilized man faced the danger of succumbing to the wild-
ness of his surroundings and reverting to savagery himself.
The pioneer, in short, lived too close to wilderness for appreciation."

In the end, much of the American wilderness was con-
quered, and between 1781 and 1976, the federal government
disposed of more than 1.1 billion acres of public domain. Of
this amount, only 287 million acres went to individual settlers
under the Homestead Act. While much of the West proved to
be too rugged for settlement by individuals schooled in East
Coast farming techniques, the resource-rich land became a
plunder playground for private enterprise. The General Land
Office was corrupt throughout its ranks and routinely made
shady deals with railroad companies and land speculators;
illegal logging and mining were rampant on public lands, and
some of America's greatest scenic wonders like Yellowstone,
Yosemite, and the Grand Canyon were gravely threatened by
private development.

Although many pioneers and/or profiteers were continuing
the quest to conquer western wilderness, an ethic of conservation was beginning to take shape in the United States
during the mid- to late 1800s. In 1872, Yellowstone became
the first national park in the world. In 1890, Yosemite,
Sequoia, and General Grant (now part of Sequoia) were also
established as national parks. The following year, Congress
passed the Forest Reserve Act, which gave the president
authority to claim an unlimited amount of public domain as
essentially off-limits to unrestricted logging, and put control
of the nation's timber and water resources back in the hands
of the federal government. The Antiquities Act of 1906, created largely in response to the pillaging of prehistoric Native
American archaeological sites in the Southwest, allowed for
the establishment of national monuments on any federal land
that the president deemed to be of "scientific, historic, or
scenic value." Within ten years, twenty national monuments

had been declared, including the Grand Canyon.

By 1900, the western frontier was essentially closed and a series of laws and agencies had been established to guard against the kinds of abuses of the public domain that had characterized the previous century. Federal programs were established to allow private interests to profit from the natural resources of the public domain. Grazing, mining, and logging on federal lands was (and still is) common practice, and it became the economic foundation of many western states.

CHAPTER 1

ALL ABOUT CAMPING

Finding a Site, Clean Campfires, Kitchen Duty

WE STAND AROUND THE CLEARING like eager medical students listening to our physician-professor course through the processes of deductive reasoning. A questionable campsite in Wyoming's Wind River Range is our test patient, and we are to diagnose its condition and, ultimately, determine whether the site should exist at all.

"It has obviously been frequently used for a long time. And it is unofficial (not a designated site of the national forest)," notes NOLS outreach manager Rich Brame, our teacher on this LNT training session. We students take these two factors under advisement as we examine the campsite in question for telling environmental and sociological symptoms. There is a big fire ring in the middle that is fortified with large, blackened rocks; a pile of branches and twigs lies next to the ring waiting for the next group of campers; the lower reaches of a few trees appear to have been stripped for wood; several logs have been placed around the fire ring as benches; and, compared to the surrounding forest, the ground is largely devoid of leaves, duff, and new plant life. We pace the perimeter of the site to complete our examination: several well-worn trails venture into surrounding thickets . . . potty paths. The size of the site appears to be getting bigger over time as people seek out new boulders and trees on which to prop packs and place equipment,

Moderately impacted campsite

Heavily impacted campsite

and there is a smaller, secondary fire ring off to the side.

We discuss the general condition of the patient. On a scale of one to five, with five being the worst, the environmental health of the campsite would be (in medical lingo) a "Code 4." But the good news is that the poor condition is stabilized and there is not much else that can happen to the site to make it any worse. And the location is not a problem; it is at least 200 feet away from a nearby lake and well off the main trail. "A lot of people have been coming here," says Brame. "If this site were to be closed, they would just camp somewhere else nearby and damage that location."

We conclude, with the help of Brame's guidance, that—although the site is not an "official" one established by land managers—the site has been established through historic use and should continue to exist in an effort to keep recreational activities in the area concentrated. We (as concerned citizens and dedicated LNT practitioners) decide the following treatment should be administered: scatter the pile of wood and dismantle the log benches to discourage large fires; pack out any trash that may make the site less appealing to prospective campers; and dismantle the secondary fire ring.

Such is the complex process of Leave No Trace camping. Like a doctor diagnosing a patient, there are often no clear-cut answers, so campers must use their best judgment in deciding, for instance, where

This heavily impacted campsite has been closed to give the land a chance to heal. (photo by David Cole)

to park their tent for the night. Armed with knowledge of the environment and an understanding of minimum-impact guidelines, the consummate LNT camper relies on reason rather than rules to make the proper choices—from deciding whether to have a fire to knowing how to keep food from curious wildlife. (For information on Leave No Trace seminars, see the appendix.)

▲ ▲ ▲

The Case for Designated Campsites

Back in the '70s when recreational use of our nation's wildlands was skyrocketing, land managers began researching and monitoring the environmental condition of campsites. They found in many popular areas across the country that it was not just the most heavily used campsites that were being turned into ecological wastelands; sites receiving only moderate use (about thirty nights per year) were also going downhill fast. For example, in Minnesota's Boundary Waters Canoe Area, the damage to most campsites went well beyond a proliferation of fire rings and soil trampling. Repeated exposure to human visitation, especially by large groups, was permanently altering the ecological communities of these areas—the rich topsoil had disappeared, leaving only nutrient-poor mineral soil; native understory plants could not survive and exotic species were taking over; mature trees were dying and young saplings did not stand a chance.

Land managers across the country—from Virginia's Shenandoah National Park to the Grand Canyon to Oregon's Eagle Cap Wilderness—adopted various strategies to deal with the problem. One of the most seemingly logical courses of action was to temporarily close overused campsites and ask visitors to pitch their tent somewhere else until the damaged areas had healed. However, it soon became obvious that it takes far longer for the land to regenerate than it does to deteriorate. So the end result of temporary campsite closures in most cases was that a larger portion of the land was disturbed than if nothing had been done at all. Such were the findings of David Cole in "Monitoring the Conditions of Wilderness Campsites," a 1983 study of temporary campsite closures at Big Lake Creek in Montana's Selway-Bitterroot Wilderness.

In 1973, approximately fifteen well-defined and environmentally damaged campsites had developed around the shore of the popular Big Lake Creek. Land managers closed seven of the sites and posted signs directing campers to alternative sites a short distance from the lake. But after eight years, vegetation recovery on the closed sites was minimal and campers had created seven new sites next to the closed areas. "The program to restore overused sites can hardly be judged a success," said the study. "In fact it was counterproductive. The major effect of the program was to increase the total area disturbed by camping by about 50 percent."

Another faulty land management approach frequently implemented by the Forest Service during the '70s and '80s was, according to Cole, relying on "dilution as the solution." Attempting to mitigate environmental impacts by encouraging campers to spread out and avoid heavily used sites was generally ineffective and just created a bigger ecological mess. Offering an analogy to the campsite dilution solution, Cole said, "We could spread our trash across the entire planet rather than concentrating it in landfills, and it would decompose faster. But more land would be impacted. And who wants to look at trash everywhere? I think we all prefer landfills."

As a result of research from Cole and others, the general consensus among land managers today is that containment is usually the best approach to managing campsite impacts. In popular wilderness areas and national parks, this is typically accomplished through permit systems in which visitors are required to camp at designated sites or zones, and/or numbers of visitors are limited by site availability. More than a quarter of our national parks now allow backcountry camping only at designated sites. And some of the most visited destinations, like Grand Canyon, Glacier, Yellowstone, Rocky Mountain, Great Smoky Mountains, and Mount Rainier National Parks, require backcountry campers to stick to fixed itineraries in which they agree to camp at a specific site each night.

Concentrating use through a system of designated campsites is unfortunate in that it requires increased regulation from land managers and generally takes away from the visitors' wilderness experience. Nevertheless, these policies must be followed in the interest of preserving wildlands for future generations and because, in most places, the rules are mandated by law. But perhaps in the future, if more campers practice Leave No Trace techniques, environmental impacts will decrease and regulations will be loosened.

"Conditions in the backcountry have either stayed the same or gotten worse because of the increased demand from visitors. We are forced to regulate things more," said Patrick Bragington, a wilderness ranger at Grand Canyon National Park, during a 1996 LNT training seminar held there. However, the bright side to the situation comes from people knowledgeable in the principles of Leave No Trace. "You cannot even tell where they camped," Bragington said.

FINDING THE PERFECT LNT CAMPSITE

If you are truly interested in protecting the environmental health of an area, keep in mind that the proverbial "perfect campsite" is not just about finding a level spot with a beautiful view and water nearby. Because the activity of camping is responsible for the majority of recreational impacts to our wildlands, where you choose to spend the night is likely the most important environmental decision you will make on a trip.

Falling under the LNT principle of "camp and travel on durable surfaces," there are three general campsite guidelines espoused by minimum-impact experts:

- When in a popular area, camp on a well-worn site to concentrate use.
- When in a rarely visited, pristine area, disperse impact by camping in a spot that has never been used before.
- Avoid sites altogether where signs of use are moderately to barely visible—this will give the land a chance to heal.
- No matter where you are, you can reduce trampling impacts to the site by wearing lightweight shoes, like sport sandals, when in camp.

And always keep in mind an LNT truism from John Hart, author of *Walking Softly in the Wilderness:* "The perfect campsite is found, not made." This means that, no matter where you decide to bed down, you should never rearrange the landscape to suit your needs—like digging up plants or rocks (little critters live under there) to create a tent pad, or moving logs and boulders around to use as camp furniture.

▲ ▲ ▲

U.S. Forest Service
Managing Timber and Trails

With roots in the 1891 Forest Reserve Act, the U.S. Forest Service was established in 1905 and is the steward of some 191 million acres of national forest and grasslands. Promoting the national forests as the "land of many uses," the Forest Service has always followed a multiple-use mandate and managed its vast reserves for the purposes of logging, mining, grazing, wildlife preservation, and recreation. Unlike other land management agencies, the Forest Service is administered by the U.S. Department of Agriculture—a branch of the federal government designed to focus on harvesting commodities rather than providing recreation. Although timber leases have historically been the agency's primary activity, the extent to which these nearly 200 million acres are used (and sometimes abused) to meet industry demands for a ready supply of lumber has varied greatly over the years.

Under the direction of the Forest Service's first agency chief, Gifford Pinchot, timber leasing policies were established to promote wise use of resources and the notion of a "sustainable yield." Conservation-oriented Forest Service managers like Aldo Leopold and Robert Marshall convinced the agency during its early days to manage some of its lands as wilderness—keeping it roadless and, essentially, unlogged. By 1939, the Forest Service had set aside 14 million acres to be preserved as "primitive areas."

However, in the decades following World War II, the postwar housing boom and American society's infatuation with a new consumerism led to rampant logging of the national forests. The agency's policy of conservation-oriented sustainable yield gave way to environmentally destructive timber quotas, which led to widespread clear-cutting practices and the subsequent destruction of watersheds and fisheries.

Between 1950 and 1959, for example, the annual timber harvest quota on national forest lands went from 3.5 billion board feet to more than 8 billion board feet. However, during that same period, the annual tally of recreation visits to national forests also increased dramatically—from 26 million to 81 million.

The Forest Service once considered recreation a secondary use in the agency's multiple-use mandate. But over the last several decades, sheer numbers have forced the agency to think—and act—otherwise. In 1995, recreation visits to national forest lands totaled nearly 830 million, up from 600 million in 1991. Encompassing more trails, campgrounds, and waterways than any other type of federally managed land, the national forests are an increasingly popular playground for all recreational users, from backpackers to mountain bikers to boaters to hunters.

On the positive side, this has helped prompt a shift in management of national forest lands away from aggressive logging practices (hiking and clear-cutting do not mix) toward policies that are aimed at pleasing the general public rather than a few timber companies.

On the downside, the growing popularity of these lands has presented land managers with a new environmental dilemma: how to keep people from loving the national forests to death. For the Forest Service, educating all kinds of users in the principles of Leave No Trace is the agency's best hope in dealing with this problem.

Choosing a Site in Popular Areas

According to Forest Service research biologist David Cole, the biggest environmental problem in wilderness areas over the past two decades is not the deterioration of popular, longtime campsites but the proliferation of new sites. Back in the 1970s, popular campsites such as horse packer camps in the River of No Return Wilderness or shelters along the Appalachian Trail looked like shantytowns. Through

Established backcountry campsite in Grand Canyon National Park
(photo by Mike Frick)

visitor education and various land management policies—primarily
restricting group size—these wilderness slums have largely disappeared, but environmental degradation caused by campers continues
to increase.

Today's wilderness travelers, it seems, are always looking for a better campsite. Even when there is a selection of suitable, established
places to pitch their tent, campers will "pioneer" a new site near existing

ones just because it is a little cleaner or more private, or has a better view. "For example, in two drainages in the Eagle Cap Wilderness," said Cole in his report "Campsites in Three Western Wildernesses" on the proliferation problem, "the number of campsites increased from 336 in 1975 to 748 in 1990."

This trend, if it were to be compared to the complexion of a typical adolescent, is like giving a wildland area a face full of acne instead of just a few unsightly large blemishes. On an individual basis, the blemishes of widespread acne may be smaller and less obnoxious than the big bull's-eye zit, but it is the quantity that leads to an unsightly appearance and scars the skin. And so it is with camping—a lot of little, seemingly innocuous sites are far more damaging to the environmental health of an area than a few well-used, visibly impacted sites.

Consequently, it is the responsibility of every Leave No Trace practitioner to sacrifice a little in the way of personal aesthetics in the interest of environmental preservation, camping in well-used sites whenever possible. With the exception of perhaps a few remote roadless areas in the West, most public lands in the Lower 48 that have trails also have an adequate supply of established campsites. You will be rewarded in minimum-impact heaven if you bite the bullet and go ahead and camp at a site that is somewhat trampled and has a few beer cans in the fire ring and toilet paper flowers in the bushes rather than bedding down at a relatively undisturbed but more scenic site nearby. Do you want to be responsible for giving the land another zit?

The perfect Leave No Trace campsite should always be located well out of view from the main trail and at least 200 feet from water sources. The best surfaces for camping are slickrock or rock outcroppings, gravel bars, and sandy beaches because they are so resistant to human impacts. Other surfaces found to be highly resilient to camper trampling are dry, grassy meadows and open forests with a grassy understory. Environments that are least resistant to human impacts are dense forests with a heavily vegetated understory of broad-leafed and woody plants.

Try to find a visibly impacted, existing site in one of these more resilient environments. Such a site is likely to have a fire ring, and ground vegetation will be worn away over most of the area, although decomposing leaves and needles will still be present in spots. Stay off sites where prior use is barely noticeable, or where use has been so severe that the soil is eroded, the ground is completely barren, and tree roots are exposed.

Choosing a Site in Pristine Areas

If you happen to be fortunate enough to be visiting a wildland area that is truly pristine—where signs of human impact are few and far between, or absent completely—then the rules of finding the perfect Leave No Trace campsite are different.

Say you are hiking cross-country in a large wilderness area in the Southwest, or in a national wildlife preserve in Alaska; it is doubtful

Pristine campsite on durable meadow, Superstition Wilderness, AZ (photo by Annette McGivney)

you will encounter a well-used campsite. In cases like this, it is better to camp at a spot that appears to have never been used before than in an area that shows just modest signs of human disturbance—like a patch of flattened grass and scattered charcoal. Make your camp on a highly durable or resilient surface, such as slickrock or a dry, grassy meadow, and only spend one night there.

Camping in a pristine area is the ultimate Leave No Trace challenge because it is imperative that you literally leave no trace—and that is very hard to do. In fact, it is impossible if you are traveling in a large group and/or have pack stock. Consequently, for those who want to camp in a large group or who plan to have several horses in camp, it is best to visit popular areas where established campsites exist.

CAMPING IN GROUPS

Although large, organized groups (of twelve or more) make up a small percentage of wildland visitors, they, in a figurative—and sometimes literal—sense, seem to scream the loudest and can have the greatest environmental impact on campsites. Group size is determined (and regulated) by land managers in most national parks and popular Forest Service wilderness areas. However, the number of people allowed to convene at a single site remains unregulated on the vast majority of wildlands, leaving it up to the good judgment of visitors to decide where and what kind of group camping is appropriate in a specific environment.

Whether it is with a Scout troop or a church group or a wilderness education program like Outward Bound or the National Outdoor Leadership School, an organized outing in the backcountry can be an extremely rewarding and enjoyable experience for the individuals involved—especially children. However, if the group is not skilled in the ways of minimum-impact camping, their outing can have devastating effects on the environment, not to mention ruin the wilderness experience of nearby campers.

How big is too big? The answer, according to NOLS research manager Chris Monz, is purely subjective. Group size is a controversial issue and the proper number varies greatly depending on who you talk to. If it is an outfitter who leads horse packing trips into Western wilderness areas, he is likely to say the common Forest Service limit of

An unnecessary fire ring is dismantled to check impact. (photo courtesy of NOLS)

twenty-five people per party is about right. However, various surveys of individual visitors to wilderness areas shows that their sense of solitude and enjoyment of their trip is significantly diminished when they encounter groups of ten or more.

"There's no research equating a specific group size with environmental impact," said Monz in a recent conversation. "[NOLS] certainly believes large groups can have a big effect, but we also believe you can mitigate that impact with responsible camping practices." Most NOLS courses lessen their environmental and social impact by breaking up into subgroups of four. Course participants travel and camp in small groups and only periodically convene in one big group.

Meanwhile, the trend among land managers in popular recreation areas is to place increasing restrictions on organized groups. In the backcountry of Canyonlands National Park, group size is limited to six; in Great Smoky Mountains it is eight; and in the Boundary Waters Canoe Area—historically a magnet for campers traveling en masse—the group size is ten, down from a previous limit of fifteen. In Grand Canyon National Park, maximum group size in the backcountry is eleven, and campers are relegated to sites designed specifically to handle quantity.

LNT Basics: Choosing a Campsite

- The perfect Leave No Trace campsite should always be located well out of view from the main trail and at least 200 feet (about 75 paces) from water sources.
- The campsite surfaces found most resistant to human impacts are slickrock or rock outcroppings; gravel bars and sandy beaches; dry, grassy meadows; and open forests with a grassy understory.

In Popular Areas

Whenever possible, park your tent at an established campsite where impact from previous campers is clearly visible.

- Established campsites typically contain a fire ring, and the ground shows signs of trampling from people and/or pack stock.
- If a site is so heavily used that the ground is barren and eroded, and tree roots are exposed, camp somewhere else so the land can heal.

In Pristine Areas

In pristine areas, where no established campsites are available, camp at a spot that appears to have never been used before rather than in an area that shows modest signs of human disturbance.

- Make your camp on a highly durable or resilient surface, such as slickrock, gravel, or a grassy meadow.
- Only camp at the pristine site for one night, and then move on.
- If you are traveling with pack stock or in a large group, avoid camping in pristine areas altogether.

CAMPFIRES—TO BURN OR NOT TO BURN

The minimum-impact battle is only half over once you find the perfect Leave No Trace campsite. Your behavior at that site—whether you are in a group or by yourself, in a pristine or a well-used location—has everything to do with how the environment will fare once you have packed up and moved on. Perhaps the most significant impact-related decision you will make is whether to have a campfire. And, if you choose to have a fire, will it be of the type that minimizes potential environmental damage?

Campfires date back, almost, to the dawn of humankind, and over the millennia, it seems our affinity for this simple natural phenomenon has never cooled. Fires have always been an integral part of the human experience in the backcountry, serving, until recently, as the primary method for cooking and staying warm. However, with today's high-tech equipment—backpacking stoves, four-season tents, ultra-insulated sleeping bags and winter apparel—people do not need fires anymore to survive when away from the comforts of civilization. Campfires now primarily meet an emotional need for nostalgia, tradition, and something comforting to stare at on a cold, dark night in the woods.

In following Leave No Trace guidelines to minimize the impact of fires in the backcountry, the simplest option is to just use a camp stove and not have a fire at all. Some people call this the "star watching" approach, because when your eyes are not glued to the glowing flames of a fire, it is much easier to appreciate all the cosmic wonders of a dark night sky. If you feel the need for a little illumination, candle lanterns work well, as do makeshift luminarias (put a few handfuls of sand in a plastic bag and anchor a small, flat candle in the center) strategically placed around camp.

There is nothing inherently wrong about having a fire when camping in the backcountry; it is a perfectly natural, and often integral, part of the outdoor experience. But as with all wildland recreational issues, the problem arises when too many people make too many fires using outdated methods, and the landscape is damaged.

Negative Impacts of Fires

Fire rings: One of the most obvious impacts of campfires is that telltale circle of rocks, to many visitors an eyesore in otherwise scenic wilderness areas that screams out to all who pass by, "Humans were here!" And, if the fortress of blackened stones was not unsightly enough, many campers seem to think the fire ring also doubles as a trash bin.

Fire rings are always a magnet for unsightly trash. (photo by Mike Frick)

All types of items that people would not toss elsewhere on the ground are thrown into the ring (beer cans are the best example), regardless of whether there is a fire going or whether the trash is even something that will burn up. Fire rings also have an amazing ability to get continually bigger, and to multiply; where there is one big daddy ring marking a backcountry campsite, you are likely to find several baby rings nearby.

Soil damage: While the charred rock menagerie of the fire ring may be unsightly, what goes on beneath the stones causes the most environmental damage. Hot fires permanently scar the landscape by altering the soil. The repeated infernos within the ring destroy organic matter and sterilize the soil as deep as 4 inches. The result is a patch of dead earth—something of a Superfund site—that will stay that way decades after the fire ring itself is gone. In popular areas where campfires are frequent, all these little dead zones can add up to a substantially altered terrain.

Consumption of fuel: The other problem with campfires is their insatiable appetite for wood. Look around a heavily used campsite in a forested setting and it is doubtful you will find any wood on the ground bigger than a twig. Then check out the surrounding trees; there is a good chance that all branches have been stripped off below 6 feet, and some younger trees may have been chopped down entirely to feed the hungry flames. This constant consumption of fuel not only impacts the health of trees and their ability to regenerate, but the absence of downed wood also takes away homes for wildlife and robs the soil of an important source of nutrients.

If there is a proliferation of campfires (especially large ones) in a wildland area over an extended period of time, the local forest ecosystem can suffer significantly. Although some people would like to believe otherwise, there is no type of environment that is less or more likely to be affected by fires; it all depends on the availability of wood, the concentration of use in the area, and the minimum-impact skills of the person building the blaze.

Yet, in light of all the potential environmental evils associated with campfires, it is also entirely possible to use Leave No Trace techniques to build a nice, cozy fire that has little or no impact on the landscape. And this is why, when it comes to discussing the issue of campfires, there is no end in sight to the debate, no right or wrong. It is sort of like the argument over abortion—some people are completely for it, others are completely against it, others say it depends on the circumstances, and all base their stance on strong personal convictions and moral values.

In October 1996 I attended a Leave No Trace training seminar held for Grand Canyon National Park staff, and the discussion about campfires was definitely the most heated of the day. As in many national parks, campfires are not allowed in the Grand Canyon backcountry, but everyone had an opinion just the same and the personal ethic regarding this combustible issue varied greatly. There was the biologist who was staunchly opposed to any kind of campfire in the wilderness and believed it an indulgent human luxury, and then there was the smokejumper who felt that as long as an abundance of "fuel" existed, it was silly to not have a fire.

How to Build a Fire the LNT Way

Evaluate local regulations and the environment: If you decide to have a fire, first make sure it is legal in the area where you are camped and consider the weather conditions—campfires can suddenly turn into wildfires when it is hot, dry, and windy.

A NOLS student perfects his mound fire–building skills.
(photo courtesy of NOLS)

Fires in popular areas: If you are staying at an established site, your campfire decision must also be based on the availability of downed wood; there should be a lot of it, not just enough for one night's inferno. The ideal low-impact fuel is loose twigs and branches that are no thicker in diameter than your wrist; never break off branches from standing trees, even if they appear dead. For car campers, the fuel availability problem is easily avoided and the environment is spared if you BYOW (bring your own wood) or—perhaps even better—invest in an artificial paraffin log, which burns longer and causes less mess than regular wood.

It is also important at established campsites to build your fire in the spot where most blazes have historically taken place. This is usually very easy to determine, because these sites are almost always marked by an enduring fire ring planted smack-dab in the center of the impacted area—just look for the beer cans.

Fires at pristine sites: When camping in a pristine area, the two best methods for building a minimum-impact fire—if there is an abundant supply of downed wood—are in a self-contained unit such as a fire pan or on a mound. When done properly, neither the pan fire nor mound fire should have any impact on the soil beneath it. However, because the business of burning inevitably attracts human activity and can become a campsite focal point, the fire should be located on a surface that is especially resistant to trampling. Gravel, sand, or slickrock are ideal.

- **The pan fire**—A technique perfected and widely used by river runners, the pan fire offers the easiest and most environmentally sensitive way to get that warm glow in the backcountry. Fire pans are simply anything that serves as a flame-resistant metal tray with sides high enough (at least 3 inches) to safely contain wood and ashes. Various common household items work fine—oil drain pans, garbage can lids, and pans from backyard barbecue grills. Now that fire pans are becoming increasingly popular among backpackers, several outdoor equipment companies have begun to market highly packable, lightweight fire pans. There is not much to making a pan fire once you have the pan—just fill the bottom with sand, gather the wood, and put it in the pan. When building the fire, prop the pan up on a few rocks to protect the surface below from any heat damage.

- **The mound fire**—This type of fire has its advantages in that you do not have to bother with packing a bulky fire pan; however, it also requires more work in camp. The tools needed are a trowel, a large stuff sack, and a ground cloth.

First, locate a source of mineral soil for building the mound; never build it on dark organic soil because this kind of dirt is rich with living organisms. Some of the best places to find mineral soil are dry streambeds where gravel or sand is easily accessible and the soil is frequently disturbed by flooding, or beneath the turned-over stump of a fallen tree.

Using the trowel, fill the large stuff sack (you can turn it inside out to keep it clean for other uses) with the mineral soil. Make a special note of your dig site so you can replace the soil when you tear down the fire. Then return to your campsite and lay down a small tarp or ground cloth (a plastic trash bag works fine) on the spot where you intend to have the fire. Spread the soil on the cloth, forming a circular, flat-topped mound about 6 to 8 inches thick. The thickness of the mound is critical in preventing any heat-caused damage to the surface beneath the ground cloth, and to keep the ground cloth itself from melting. The circumference of the mound should be larger than the fire to allow for the inevitable spread of coals.

As with all campfires, both pan and mound fires should be kept small, using only small scraps of wood for fuel. And the wood should be burned all the way down to a fine ash to eliminate the lingering presence of charcoal. When you are ready to pack up camp, make sure the fire is completely out and then scatter the leftover ashes across a broad area away from the campsite (the ashes should be cool enough for you to run your hand through). If you built a mound fire, return the mineral soil to its original location.

THE CAMP KITCHEN

There may not be a sink and fridge, but the so-called "kitchen" area of a campsite is the same kind of magnet for social activity and mess making as your kitchen at home. However, unlike what goes on in your private abode, the backcountry kitchen is shared with all the previous and future campers at the site—and with all wildlife living in the area. A messy kitchen spells problems, not only for you, but for people who follow you, as well as for numerous species of birds and animals that can come to depend on scrounging for scraps rather than hunting for food.

A friend of mine once spent the night with five ornery black bears because he unknowingly set up camp at an established backcountry site in eastern Arizona that had become the domain of bruin bandits. A long history of messy kitchen practices by backcountry visitors was to blame for the transformation of the wild bears into habituated camp robbers. As soon as my friend and his three buddies dropped off their packs at the site and headed downriver to go fishing, the bears moved in—probably just as they did with all campers at that site.

When my friend and his companions returned later that afternoon, they found the clan of five bears tearing apart their packs and eating the contents. They tried scaring the bruins away from the site, but the

Rock is an ideal durable surface for the LNT kitchen. (photo courtesy of NOLS)

highly habituated animals did not budge. The bears continued to occupy the campsite, pillaging the area into the night. When they were done with the packs, they moved on to the bear-bagged food suspended from a tree branch and devoured that; then they pawed at the trash in the fire ring and ate the contents of a fishing tackle box. Meanwhile, my friend and his fellow campers had to spend the night on the cold ground across the stream from their occupied campsite, watching the raid from afar. The next morning, when the bears finally left the site— full of pancake mix, sausage, lead sinkers, and nylon cordura—my friend and his buddies picked up the tattered remains of their gear and hiked out with a new respect for what sloppy camp habits can do to wildlife.

Preparing Before You Leave Home

- Minimize mess in the camp kitchen by repackaging your food before leaving home. Take food items out of their boxes, wrappers, and cans and place them in meal-sized portions in resealable plastic bags to cut down on trash and help prevent you from cooking more grub than you want to eat.
- Plan your meal portions correctly so that you do not have to worry about icky leftovers. To this end, one-pot meals are the simplest to prepare, eat, and clean up.
- Stay away from greasy, aromatic foods. This will minimize the mess and avoid attracting wildlife.

Choosing a Location

- Find a spot for the kitchen that is well away from tents and trails, and 200 feet from water sources.

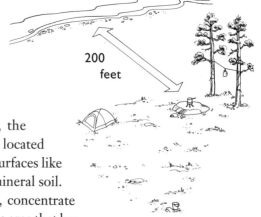

200
feet

- At a pristine campsite, the cooking area should be located on trampling-resistant surfaces like a rock outcropping or mineral soil.
- At an existing campsite, concentrate use by cooking within the area that has

been previously used and is visibly impacted rather than on the periphery.
- Try to find a spot that is relatively free of debris so that if you accidentally drop food waste or trash it will be easily visible.

Food Handling

The key to a clean camp is a clean kitchen. Here are a few pointers to help you minimize your environmental impact and keep unwanted visitors out of camp:
- When cooking and eating, pay close attention to and retrieve any pieces of food (even crumbs) that may drop on the ground.
- Food scraps, as well as any uneaten leftovers, should never be buried; animals will dig up your dinner discards as soon as you vacate the site (or sooner).
- Food wastes should be packed out with other garbage.

Doing the Dishes

When you are finished dining (and have eaten every last bite), do not waste any time in cleaning up, because the longer you wait, the more food particles stick to pans. The recommended Leave No Trace method for doing the dishes is to wash them with hot water and a scrubbing sponge; soap presents a potential environmental hazard and is not necessary to get dishes clean, especially if you avoid using greasy foods. After the meal, pour a little water in the dirty pot, heat it on the stove, and then take the pan to the cleanup area and scrub. There are two ways you can responsibly dispose of the "gray water," depending on which is easier for you to stomach.

Straining: The first method is to strain the water to remove the food particles; pour slowly through a small strainer, coffee filter, bandanna, or even your fingers. This is probably what you will prefer to do with the water after you've washed a dirty pot. These remaining tiny food scraps should be packed out in your trash bag, and the waste water should be scattered in the bushes or poured into a sump (pit) well away from the campsite and 200 feet from any water sources.

Drinking: The other option is to send the liquid down the human hatch. Rinse the dish you ate out of and drink the water. It is, after all,

Straining dishwater for proper disposal (photo courtesy of NOLS)

just a little bit more of the food you ate, mixed with warm water—kind of an after-dinner broth. I have periodically partaken of this broth on backcountry outings, and it is not so bad. However, if the idea does not strike your fancy, do not hesitate to use the strain-and-scatter or sump method instead.

PEACEFUL COEXISTENCE WITH WILDLIFE

You can be fastidiously clean with food waste in your camp kitchen, but keeping area wildlife from turning into junk-food junkies also requires that you carefully store your food. Although black bears are, perhaps, the most notorious for learning to associate camping and backpacking equipment with the source of their next meal, the natural habits of many different species can be altered if they learn to pillage and panhandle. In established camping areas in popular national parks, you are likely to be visited by a variety of critters—raccoons, squirrels, chipmunks, skunks, deer—all looking for a handout. In a few national parks that I have visited in the Southwest, I have even seen buzzards swoop down and pick apart a box of Pop Tarts as if it were roadkill, and I have been surrounded by feral cows that were very set on nibbling at my backpack.

Avoid Handouts

No matter how cute the begging tactics of these critters, refrain from feeding wildlife. They are, after all, supposed to be wild, and the animals' very survival is jeopardized if they lose their instinctive ability to fend for themselves. Once bears gone bad become habitual campsite raiders, land managers will typically relocate the bruins, and if that does not work, they are often given the death sentence.

Secure All Food and Other Attractants

The best way to protect your food and gear—and the future of area wildlife—is to secure all your food, garbage, and any scented toiletries (like toothpaste, sunscreen, and lip balm). In some areas, bearproof containers are provided for this purpose. In most areas, especially the backcountry, you will have to hang your food in "bear-bag" fashion. Check with land managers before visiting an area to find out how elaborate your bear-bagging suspension system should be. Here are some general guidelines for keeping your edibles out of the reach of wildlife:

- You will need anywhere from 30 to 100 feet of nylon rope and a sturdy bag or stuff sack to hold all the goods.
- As a general rule, food should be hung from a tree (or trees) about 100 feet from your tent site. And it is best to hang the food bag near the camp kitchen in an effort to keep appetizing odors concentrated in one area.
- If bear raids have not been reported, or if you know you are not in bear country, simply slinging a rope over a lofty branch and tying the bag to it will keep it out of reach of most critters.
- If you are in bear country, or especially an area where bears have been raiding campsites, spend a little bit more time rigging up the food bag so that it is suspended (about 15 feet high) between two trees (at least 23 feet apart). This will decrease the likelihood that a black bear will try to steal your food by climbing the tree from which its prospective dinner is dangling. (However, in the case of

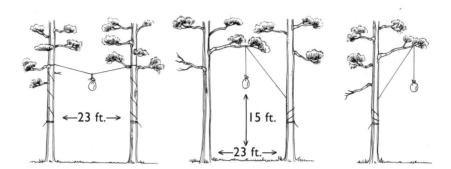

my friend who shared his camp with five bears, the bruins simply broke off the entire branch that the food bag was tied to.)

Be Aware of Water Sources

Regardless of whether any furry bandits enter your camp or whether you see any animals at all, be sensitive to the fact that your temporary presence inevitably impacts area wildlife. If you are camped near a water source (at least 200 feet away, of course), try to minimize the disruption you may cause to wildlife watering habits by visiting the spring or stream only once. This can be most easily accomplished if you pack a collapsible water jug, then take it with you to the water source and pump or extract all the water you will need in camp in one visit, rather than make repeated trips to what is undoubtedly a critical spot for wildlife.

TAKING OUT THE TRASH

The "pack it in; pack it out" Leave No Trace principle is probably the most universally accepted part of today's minimum-impact wilderness etiquette. What is there not to understand? Simply, do not litter... everything that you take with you into the backcountry, from chewing gum to gear, you must take out.

However, this LNT principle involves more than just the "do not be a litterbug" decree. It has to do with making the backcountry a better place when you leave than it was when you entered. That means not only packing out your own trash, but picking up and carrying out other people's garbage, sprucing up campsites, and dismantling unnecessary fire rings.

Garbage Die-hards

One devoted practitioner of the "pack it out" principle is longtime NOLS instructor Del Smith, who played an instrumental role in getting the present-day Leave No Trace program started. Smith delights in packing out other people's trash, and she and her NOLS students are responsible for tidying up many a popular wilderness area. In camp and on the trail, Smith scours the ground for what she calls "microtrash"—teeny-weeny pieces of paper, polypropylene fuzz balls, cigarette butts. And she also keeps her eyes peeled for discarded junk; if the item will not fit in her pack, she straps it to the outside. "My house is filled with junk that I have hauled out," she said in a recent conversation. "Once I packed out a linoleum tabletop, and another time I strapped an old bale of chicken wire to my pack."

Smith is not alone in her fetish for found items; most NOLS field instructors can recount numerous odd forms of garbage they have hauled from the backcountry. Longtime field instructor Tim Wilson recalled packing out pieces of an airplane and a complete chain saw. "I once packed out three ¾-inch iron pipes that were each about 6 feet long," reported NOLS outreach manager Rich Brame in a 1996 LNT training session. "It took five days, but, fortunately, there was not much lightning at the time."

Smith and other NOLS instructors admit they do not expect the average minimum-impact camper to crawl around on hands and knees looking for cigarette butts or to haul a 20-pound piece of junk out of the wilderness. It is essential, however, that you pay close attention to the goings-on of trash when you are in the backcountry.

Leaving a Clean Campsite

- Keep track of your own garbage by stashing it all in one bag, and stow the bag in a handy place in your pack so you can immediately get rid of discarded items instead of putting them in a pocket, only to be accidentally pulled out and blown away later. A plastic sack the size and weight of a bread bag works well for carrying garbage.
- When you are ready to leave a campsite, inspect the ground after you have packed all your gear to make sure you did not inadvertently leave some small item hidden in the grass or buried in the sand.

- When vacating a campsite in a pristine area, put some effort into erasing all signs of your stay there: fluff the grass where the tent was located, fill in tent-stake holes, and use a fallen pine branch to sweep dirt and sand clean of footprints.
- If you are leaving an impacted site in a popular camping area, try to make the site look as appealing as possible so future visitors will not be inclined to move on to a less-impacted site. Pick up all trash and clean out the main fire ring. If there are smaller, secondary fire rings at the site, these should be dismantled—grind charcoal down and scatter ashes in the bushes a good distance away from the site, throw any excess wood into the forest, and take the rocks from the ring and place them (black side down) throughout the area.

When Smith dismantles a fire ring, she even goes the extra mile and revegetates the scarred spot with organic soil and a few carefully transplanted plants from nearby. "Although it is dirty work, dismantling a fire ring and restructuring a site is really fun. Some people may think I am crazy," she added, contemplating her environmental zealousness. "But I find that Leave No Trace ethics has a spiritual side to it."

LNT Basics: A Low-Impact Camp

Campfires

- Choose to not have a fire, and instead rely on a modern backpacking stove for cooking and on good clothing, a tent, and a well-insulated sleeping bag for staying warm and dry.
- If you decide to have a fire, first make sure it is legal in the area where you are camped and that there is no danger of it starting a wildfire.
- Make sure plenty of downed wood is available for fuel. The ideal low-impact fuel is loose twigs and branches that are no thicker in diameter than your wrist; never break off branches from standing trees, even if they appear dead.
- At established campsites, build your fire in the primary fire ring to concentrate impact.

- In a pristine area where there is no fire ring, build a minimum-impact fire in a self-contained unit such as a fire pan or on a mound.
- Eliminate unsightly charcoal by burning wood all the way down to ash. Once the fire is out, scatter the ash.

The Camp Kitchen

- At a pristine site, the cooking area should be located on trampling-resistant surfaces like a rock outcropping or mineral soil.
- At an existing site, concentrate use by cooking within the area that is visibly impacted, rather than on the periphery.
- Keep a clean camp by avoiding dropping food on the ground and by packing out all food wastes.
- Consider rinsing bowl with hot water and drinking the broth—good for the environment and good for rehydration.
- Wash dirty pots with hot water and a scrubbing sponge; avoid using soap. Strain gray water and scatter or dump it in a sump well away from the campsite and 200 feet from any water sources.

Avoid Impacting Wildlife

- Never give wildlife a handout.
- Hang or secure all food, garbage, and scented items to avoid habituating area wildlife.
- Minimize trips to the water source.

Leave a Clean Camp

- Pack out all your trash, as well as litter left behind by others. Keep track of all your garbage by storing it in a single bag.
- Reduce trampling by wearing lightweight, flat-soled shoes like sport sandals or running shoes when in camp.
- A lightweight backpacking tent is much easier on the ground than the old-fashioned canvas variety.
- Dismantle secondary fire rings at established campsites.
- Fluff up the grass and fill in tent-stake holes when vacating a pristine campsite.

CHAPTER 2

WASTE NOT, WANT NOT

▬

LNT Principles of Hygiene and the Wilderness Bathroom

SOME SMELLS STAY WITH YOU FOREVER—especially the nauseating kind. There is one such odor that permanently resides in my memory, thanks to a backpacking trip I took on a section of the Appalachian Trail in Virginia.

I was hiking as part of an organized trip, and we were camped at a well-used site that was designated for groups of AT hikers. It was dusk in our little tent city when I followed a short side trail into the bushes to find a private spot to pee. I did my business, washed my hands, and then went back to the campsite to help prepare dinner. Sitting in front of my tent, fumbling through my food bag, I smelled something strange, something truly putrid. It was coming from my boot.

The sun had set, but there was still enough light to see what was plastered across the bottom of my shoe: human shit. It was fresh, so the feces smelled ripe and was thoroughly smushed into every groove on my boot sole. Apparently some inconsiderate person who had probably stayed at the group campsite the previous evening did not care to properly dispose of his or her waste—or, at the very least, to walk a decent distance from camp to do the deed.

Certainly, there are many other substances that are more toxic to humans and the environment than human poop; smelly excreta are a natural by-product of all warm-blooded beings. But there is something about encountering human feces in the backcountry—seeing it, smelling it, and, especially, stepping in it—that is truly repulsive and can ruin a person's "wilderness experience" like nothing else. A visible buildup of people poop—and usually the accompanying toilet paper—in popular wildland areas is a danger to public health, but the thing that stinks the most is what it does to a beautiful backcountry destination on an aesthetic level.

If we are to have any clean and intact recreational lands left at all—especially the "untrammeled" kind defined in the 1964 Wilderness Act—we human visitors have to treat the land with respect and not as a dumping ground. According to a key principle of the Leave No Trace ethic, we have to "properly dispose of what we cannot pack out." That means dealing with our poop rather than ignoring it, not leaving toilet paper behind, and making sure our personal hygiene practices do not negatively impact the environment.

▲ ▲ ▲

Weird Science
Digging up Dirt on Human Waste in the Backcountry

Unlike campsite impacts or trampling on trails, human waste is not a popular topic among research biologists. There are, nevertheless, a few iron-stomached souls who have conducted limited research on the subject.

One such effort took place in the 1970s and was part of a wilderness impact study commissioned by the Sierra Club. The nonprofit environmental organization wanted to find out what impact its organized "Sierra Club Outings" backcountry trips were having on California's Sierra Nevada mountains.

To that end, a group of researchers observed (from afar) the defecation practices of Sierra Club Outings participants—most of whom were traveling in large groups and using latrines to do their business. The group leader would usually determine where the latrine was dug, and the big hole was then the receptacle of all the group's poop for, in most cases, less than twenty-four hours. The researchers made a note of all these latrine sites scattered across the Sierras, then they went back anywhere from one to three years later and uncovered the stinking deposits to see how the feces was faring.

Those doing the digging and subsequent observing were all surprised to find that the buried treasure, along with many of its resident bacterial cooties, was alive and well and had decomposed very little—if at all. "The commonplace assumptions about decomposition are simply not borne out by the actual unearthing of latrines, even after one or two years," said the report on the foul findings, noting that the popular assumption among "public health authorities" was that latrine contents generally decompose in a month or two. "No pronounced evidence of putrefaction was found. The material looked more or less like surface privy excreta, and it still possessed the typical odor of old excreta."

Another study conducted about a decade later in Montana's Bridger Range unearthed the same stinking truths—except this time the primary fecal focus was on cat holes. Researchers from Montana State University in Bozeman buried bacteria-rich deposits of human poop in cat holes that varied in depth from 2 to 8 inches and were located in six different types of Rocky Mountain soil environments and elevations. When the samples were dug up fifty-one weeks later, after one winter had passed, all the feces remained a virtual playground for various disease-causing bacteria (namely *E. Coli* and salmonella).

"The idea that shallow burial renders feces harmless in a short time is fallacious," said a report from the researchers titled "Potential Health Hazards from Human Wastes in Wilderness." The report continued: "Site did not make the difference we expected. The results seemed to apply to all elevations and exposures on this mountain." The researchers went on to conclude: "From our data, it is unrealistic to hope for a rapid die-off of intestinal bacteria in cat holes. Pathogens might be transferred to later campers in three ways: by direct contact with feces, by insects, or by water." Both studies pointed out, however, that putting poop in a cat hole was preferable to a latrine because the smaller the fecal deposit, the greater its contact with surrounding soil organisms and air, which are central to the decomposition process.

Meanwhile, backcountry visitors can at least take solace in knowing that their urine is pretty benign. In the United States, human urine may smell rank when it accumulates in an urban back alley, but it is seldom the carrier of any serious micro-cooties that feces is. As for its impact to wildlands, one industrious graduate student in California conducted research on how urine affected subalpine plants in the Sierras. Daniel Holmes concluded, after pouring 200-milliliter doses of urine over twenty-one different plant species, that "the extent of urine damage to plants in backcountry camp areas appears insufficient to be considered important in [land] management."

The study did document, however, that human pee caused leaf damage and browning on some plants. And a potentially detrimental indirect impact is that certain animals are attracted to the salt in our urine, and they will quickly eat up plants that we have doused with pee.

WASTE MANAGEMENT ON PUBLIC LANDS

As a result of the burgeoning visitation trends in wildland areas over the last several decades, problems with poop proliferation and other human wastes pose a significant challenge to land managers.

The World Health Organization estimates that the average adult produces about one liter—some two pounds' worth—of excreta (half of that is the solid kind) per day. For the sake of discussion, consider that Great Smoky Mountains National Park counted more than 100,000 backcountry overnight stays in 1995. If most of those visitors stayed in the park for twenty-four hours, that means more than 100 tons of human poop and pee was bequeathed upon the Smokies' backcountry in twelve months. That is, literally, a shitload of waste, considering most of it probably never left the park by means of a sewer system and, instead, lurks at this very moment beneath a shallow grave in a half million different burial spots.

Outhouses Are In

In order to prevent the spread of disease from fecal pathogens and to reduce the chance that visitors will step in each other's crap, many popular national parks and wilderness areas now have outhouses or vault toilets in the vicinity of backcountry campgrounds and trailheads. According to various surveys of land managers, these established toilets can be found at about half of all national park backcountry campsites and in 40 percent of wilderness areas.

Backpacking all day through a wilderness area, only to find a smelly portable toilet at your designated campsite, can be somewhat disconcerting. But such is the reality of wilderness travel in a world where, in the words of NOLS outreach manager Rich Brame during a 1996 LNT training seminar, "Wildlands are finite, and people are infinite."

Understanding and Avoiding Potential Health Hazards

Beyond the fact that backcountry visitors do not want to see or smell people turds and urine, not much is known about how our wastes affect wildland environments. It is easy to assume that if you cannot see waste, then the environmental and public health hazards are gone as well, but research suggests otherwise. The few studies that have been done on the unseemly subject have uncovered the following truths (see this chapter's sidebar Weird Science for all the gory details):

- Human feces buried in a group latrine can take more than three years to decompose.
- Pathogens in human feces buried in shallow cat holes can remain a potential health hazard for at least a year.
- Human urine can brown leaves and attract animals but, generally, it is not a health hazard.

Use a privy whenever one is available to concentrate waste in the backcountry. (photo by David Cole)

Although you are more likely to get sick from eating a meal in a restaurant that was prepared by someone with cootie-laden hands than from exposure to human poop in the backcountry, even our nation's most pristine wilderness areas are not disease-free. A protozoa called *Giardia lamblia* inhabits most wildland waterways, and both humans and animals can be on the receiving or giving end of this fecal-to-oral-transmitted pathogen. When humans are stricken with giardiasis, they typically find it a gut-wrenching experience characterized by lots of diarrhea and nausea. Less powerful bacteria and viruses also inhabit backcountry waters and can cause intestinal afflictions in humans (often known as "Trekker's Trots"), as can poor hygiene practices among fellow campers.

What this all boils down to is the need for understanding basic differences between places where there are flush toilets and water faucets and places where there are not. In order to avoid becoming ill from fecal-borne cooties when visiting the sewerless backcountry:

• Purify water before drinking it.
• Wash your hands after doing the deed and before preparing food.
• Give your solid wastes a proper burial.

▲ ▲ ▲

National Park Service
Aiming to Please All Kinds of Visitors

While the management objectives of the National Park Service are not split by a multiple-use mandate as are those of the Forest Service or the Bureau of Land Management, the agency is nonetheless divided with a dual mission that is inherently contradictory. Created in 1916 by the National Parks Organic Act, the Park Service is charged with preserving our nation's crown jewels as well as enabling people to enjoy them. On the one hand, this means keeping parklands in a primitive state and undisturbed by human development. On the other hand, it means building roads, restaurants, campgrounds, and trails to accommodate the desires of the average American tourist.

From the remote 13-million-acre Wrangell–St. Elias National Park in Alaska to the White House in Washington, D.C., the Park Service manages a wide variety of national treasures—a total of 355 "units" in all. However, much of the 80 million acres of federal land placed under the agency's stewardship is found in its 54 national parks and 74 national monuments. These preserves generally have more recreation restrictions than Forest Service lands; they rarely allow mountain bikes or dogs on trails and a permit must be obtained for overnight stays in the backcountry. But, like the national forests, our national parks and monuments have experienced significant increases in visitation over the last few decades, and many wilderness areas are suffering from overuse. Recreation visits to National Park Service units in 1995 totaled nearly 270 million, up from 216 million in 1985.

Visitation at national parks, however, is highly concentrated, with 28 percent of all visitors going to the ten most popular units. Among these most visited sites are Great Smoky Mountains and Grand Canyon National Parks, Blue Ridge Parkway, and Lake Mead National Recreation Area.

But while Grand Canyon National Park, for example, received more than 4.5 million visitors in 1996, nearby Pipe Springs National Monument (also in Arizona) saw only 4,000 visitors. The discrepancy between the units in revenues raised by visitor entrance fees is the source of great debate. In short, many park units cannot cover their operating costs solely through visitation and need to be subsidized by the federal government to stay open.

Conservative members of Congress have proposed closing park units that cannot pay for themselves. Meanwhile, national park advocates have been pushing lawmakers to allocate more money to the Department of the Interior budget to pay for the upkeep of our national treasures.

While no resolution is in sight, the National Park Service is currently experimenting with an increased fee system at the most popular units to raise badly needed revenue for the agency. In 1997, for example, the admission fee to Grand Canyon and Yosemite National Parks doubled from $10 to $20 per vehicle.

Whether the increased fee system will solve all the National Park Service's problems is doubtful. In the end, preservation of our parks will require lawmakers to see past the issue of dollars and cents and remember why these special places were set aside in the first place.

THE SCOOP ON WHAT TO DO WITH YOUR POOP

Comfortably and responsibly disposing of our own feces in the backcountry is, for many people, the most difficult part of the Leave No Trace program, because it is a "lost art," in the words of Kathleen Meyer, author of *How to Shit in the Woods*. "Generally, a city-bred adult can expect to be no more successful than a tottering one-year-old in dropping his or her pants to squat," wrote Meyer. "Shitting in the woods is an acquired rather than innate skill, a skill honed only by practice, a skill all but lost to the bulk of the population, along with the arts of making soap, carding wool, and skinning buffalo."

Plan Ahead

As part of your preparation for any backcountry trip, come up with a poop plan. Maybe this is something you can take for granted in the city, but anticipating how you are going to dispose of your waste in the wilds, and bringing along the necessary tools to successfully accomplish the mission, makes the whole process less stressful, more efficient, and, dare I say, reasonably enjoyable.

First, contact the appropriate land manager and find out what the rules are regarding waste disposal in the area you will be visiting. If you are camping or hiking in an area where toilets are provided, hold your nose and use them. In these places, land managers have decided that heavy visitation warrants the installation of a toilet because it is better to concentrate the waste in one strategically located spot than to have campers digging up each other's cat holes.

Some people like the convenience of having an established place to poop located a short walk from their tent; others feel the man-made intrusion interferes with their wilderness experience. If you do not like the idea of doing your business in an outhouse and would rather gaze out at a beautiful panorama when answering nature's call, then steer clear of heavily visited backcountry destinations. Most parks and wilderness areas that require visitors to obtain a permit and camp at designated sites are likely to have designated toilets as well.

If outhouses or vault toilets are not provided, chances are the management policy is for campers to dig a cat hole and to pack out their toilet paper. Other methods used in special circumstances include packing out the poop, digging a latrine, smearing (also called surface disposal), and something known as a "shit put," where the goods are deposited on a rock and hurled into the abyss—usually off a glacier. (For more information on appropriate alternative waste-disposal methods for specific types of users or environments, refer to chapters 3, The Wilderness on Foot, 4, Riding Softly in the Saddle, 5, Minimizing Impacts on Waterways, and 6, Special Environments.)

According to Leave No Trace guidelines, there are three main objectives to consider when deciding how and where to dispose of your poop:

- Minimize the chance that other people and/or animals will find it.
- Minimize the chance that nearby waters could be polluted.
- Maximize the rate of decomposition.

The Art of the Cat Hole

The cat-hole route is the most widely used and the best option if you are not certain about which disposal method to use. When using a cat hole, the key to achieving pooping perfection is, as in real estate sales, location . . . location . . . location.

For starters, the cat hole should be located at least 200 feet from any water sources, campsites, and trails. But there are also some aesthetic factors to consider when deciding where to dig: the site should entertain the squatter with an inspiring view (anything from a quiet forest scene to a sweeping mountain panorama); it should be intensely private, without any worries of being spotted by other humans; and it must be comfortable—not on a steep slope or swarming with fire ants, for example. Additionally, maximum conditions for decomposition will be achieved if the hole is dug in organic soil (rich in microorganisms) and in a spot that is somewhat moist but receives a fair amount of sunlight.

Now, after taking a short morning hike to get your bowels moving and to find the prime cat-hole site, it is time to dig the hole. You will need some kind of trowel—there is the standard orange plastic shovel, which has been known to break in rocky or frozen ground; a basic gardening trowel will do; or you can purchase a stainless-steel shovel with a collapsible handle and sturdy carrying case, called the "Cadillac

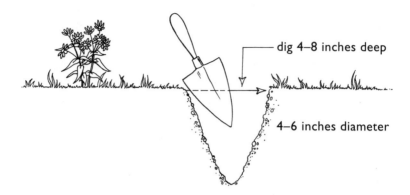

dig 4–8 inches deep

4–6 inches diameter

of trowels" by *BACKPACKER* magazine. The cat hole should be about 4 to 8 inches deep, and 4 to 6 inches in diameter.

Some people are natural squatters; others have a hard time relaxing and holding their balance when straddling a small hole. If you are one of the latter, try sitting on a fallen log (look out for the ants) or on a flat-topped rock, and hang your buns off the end, resting strategically above the hole you just dug. Or hold on to a sturdy branch or rock when in the squatting stance, to take the pressure off your legs. However, hold on tight because there is nothing worse than losing your balance and falling backward into the hole after you have made a deposit.

Once you have done the deed, throw a little soil in the hole for good measure and stir the stuff with a stick to speed up decomposition, and throw the stick in too. Then use your trowel to place at least 2 inches of topsoil back in the hole and camouflage the excavation site. (Diluting poop with a little water from your water bottle may help minimize smelly problems.)

When to Make a Latrine

Although dispersing buried fecal waste across a broad area through the use of cat holes is generally preferable to concentrating it in a latrine, sometimes digging a big poop pit may be your best option. This is the case, for example, if you are camping with a group of children and you know they do not have the ability to properly dig their own cat holes—and somehow you neglected to pick a campsite with an outhouse. Or, if you are camping in a popular backcountry site with no outhouse, with a group that will be staying at that spot for more than one or two nights, a latrine may be appropriate.

Dig the latrine when you first get to camp and make sure everyone knows where it is. The hole must be at least 200 feet from any water sources or drainages, and should be wider than it is deep—and at least 1 foot deep. Make the hole rectangular-shaped so it accommodates squatting. Or, if your group has the packing capacity, bring in some type of toilet seat device to place over the hole. Soil should be thrown in the hole after each use, and the latrine should be covered up with dirt when the waste accumulation is within 4 to 6 inches of the surface.

If you anticipate that you may be in a situation where digging a latrine would be necessary, consider the better minimum-impact option of camping in an area where outhouses are provided, or bring along a portable group potty (see Canoeing and Rafting in chapter 5, Minimizing Impacts on Waterways, for more details on these products).

Surface Disposal

Surface disposal—commonly known as smearing—was all the rage among LNT aficionados in the early '90s. This unlikely method involves pooping on a flat, inorganic surface, such as slickrock, and then spreading it across the surface with a stick or stone, as if you are icing a cake. This modus operandus came into vogue as the result of field observations that showed that feces exposed to sunlight and warmth decomposed and virtually disappeared within several days. But the folks who pioneered this approach to pooping also emphasized that one should only engage in smear tactics in extremely remote locations, well away from trails, and where there is a very dry, sunny climate—like in the Southwest desert, in the Rockies above tree line, or in the northern reaches above the Arctic Circle, where the ground (if you can get to it) is too frozen for digging.

"The smearing issue is a vexing one," contemplated NOLS research biologist Chris Monz in a recent conversation. "For a while, many wilderness travelers were smearing, but now we believe cat holes are almost always the better way to go." The more that people got into smearing, the more reports surfaced from backcountry visitors—especially in the desert Southwest—of rocks frosted with something disgusting and brown. Aside from the aesthetic consequences, smearing also poses health risks for those who follow in the footsteps of the smearer; fecal pathogens can be picked up and transported by insects, carried on the wind, or washed by rain or snowmelt into waterways. There are places where this type of surface disposal may, nevertheless, meet LNT objectives more effectively than burial, but such locations are few and far between.

Packing It Out

In places where waste burial is not possible or environmentally advantageous, packing out your poop may the best (or only available) evacuation route. On many popular whitewater rivers in the West, like the Colorado River through Grand Canyon National Park, land management policy dictates that all solid wastes be carried out via portable potties. Climbers in Yosemite National Park and hikers through the narrows of Zion National Park are also required to pack it out, and typically do it using a simple PVC pipe contraption called a "poop tube" (see Sea Kayaking in chapter 5, Minimizing Impacts on Waterways, for more details on this ingenious device).

Even if packing it out is not required by land managers, there may be some places where, because of high visitation or an extremely sensitive environment, you decide that taking your waste with you rather than leaving it behind is the most responsible thing to do. Such is the case for some LNT-minded kayakers traveling the Maine Island Trail who want to minimize human impacts on the tiny barrier islands where paddlers camp. Many of these poop packers have pioneered their own techniques—like using a Tupperware container and kitty litter, or a system of poop-filled paper bags stored in resealable plastic bags (see Waste Disposal in the Sea Kayaking section of chapter 5 for more information). Keep in mind, however, that no matter how you pack it, all poop must ultimately be deposited (without the plastic bags and/or containers) in a proper human-waste-disposal site—such as an RV dump station or outhouse.

TP, PEE, AND OTHER HYGIENIC HANG-UPS

Certainly, knowing how to effectively deal with your poop is the major hurdle when it comes to backcountry hygiene, but there are other concerns as well when traveling in a world without plumbing. For instance, what about wiping?

The Tissue Issue

In our everyday, flushable environs, toilet paper is part and parcel of the evacuation process. However, in the backcountry, it poses an environmental dilemma. You should not bury it, because it decomposes very slowly and animals like to dig it up. You should not burn it because land managers will tell you that more wildfires have been started by flaming TP than they care to count. This leaves two responsible minimum-impact options when it comes to the tissue issue: either pack it out, or leave it at home and use wipes provided by nature.

Disgusting toilet paper "flowers" just off the trail (photo courtesy of NOLS)

Natural wipes:

river stone

seaweed

snow

moss

fir cone

large leaf

The whole business of toilet paper is entirely discretionary. After all, people were pooping long before double-quilted TP was invented. But on the other hand, our modern-day bottoms have been conditioned since birth to be well wiped, and slacking off in this area can lead to uncomfortable skin irritations.

Traveling sans TP does not mean you should abandon the practice of wiping, but that you should become an educated user of the many tissue alternatives available in the great outdoors. I know many people who are enthusiastic connoisseurs of natural wiping materials: in desert and river environs, one hiker swears by palm-sized, smooth sandstone; another friend, who spends more time in the mountains, sings the praises of fallen leaves, and when they are available in abundant quantities, he will enjoy the luxurious pampering of a woolly mullein leaf or two. Other organic options include snowballs, soft cones from fir trees, and seaweed. As a general minimum-impact rule, it is best to reach for something that is already on the ground instead of defoliating a live plant. When you are done wiping, put whatever it is you used into the cat hole to be buried with the rest of your offerings.

If experimenting with nature's various tissue alternatives does not appeal to you, the "mitten method" is a tidy way to keep soiled TP out of the backcountry—and it keeps you from having to touch it. For packing out toilet paper using this hands-off approach, you will need a well-stocked supply of medium-sized, open-top plastic sandwich bags and one large resealable bag.

After doing your duty in the cat hole and replacing the soil, use a conservative amount of TP (you still have to pack it out) and throw it on the ground. Then take one of the open-top plastic bags and invert

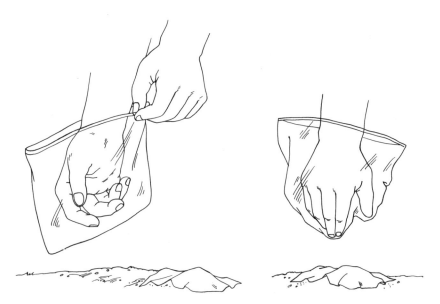

it like a mitten over your hand. Pick up the toilet paper, using the "mitten," and pull the bag right-side out over the soiled tissue. The tissue is now in its own self-contained storage unit; place it inside the large resealable bag. If you really want to improve the aesthetics of the process, use an opaque resealable bag for storing the TP so you do not have to look at it, and occasionally use a perfumed towelette to hide the smell of the TP stash. Then carry all your TP supplies in their own designated ditty bag so you will know what you are pulling out of your pack. No one wants to get their TP bag when they thought they were reaching for lunch.

Women's Hygiene

For menstruating women, the mitten method—or a less elaborate baggie system—suffices to pack out tampons and other items. Carrying these out of the backcountry is the only responsible LNT option and, although it may seem like an unpleasant hassle at first, once you get a system down, it will become second nature. Perfumed towelettes are especially handy during these times for cleaning purposes and for keeping the stash in the baggie smelling fresh. Other methods for absorbing odors include placing a crushed aspirin or used tea bag (herbal or black will do) in the stuff being packed out.

Baby Diapers

If you happen to have a baby along, regardless of your diaper prefer-
ences, scrape off as much poop as possible with a stick and bury it in a
cat hole. Be prepared to pack out all of the disposable diapers. If you
are using nondisposables, wash them out 200 feet away from water
sources. Rinsing the diapers can be problematic because they will contaminate the rinse container you use, but this is no excuse to contaminate a water source. Just carry the poopy rinse container in a secured
plastic bag and keep it away from all food and utensils.

A Few Pointers About Pee

Compared to human waste concerns of the solid kind, peeing in the
backcountry is a simple affair. Human urine in the well-vaccinated
United States poses minimal threats in terms of disease, and it is quickly
absorbed into the soil where it is deposited. However, when picking a
place to pee, keep in mind that animals are attracted to the salts in our
urine and if you happen to water some plants, critters will soon come
and defoliate them. (Diluting urine with a little water from your water
bottle may help minimize salty problems.) Also, avoid peeing in areas
where others might camp.

Men have it easiest: just aim with the wind and keep the spray away
from vegetation and trails. Women, meanwhile, must squat and be
concerned with not splattering their boots. I have found that sand or
a bed of pine needles absorbs the force of oncoming liquid with little
or no repercussions. In any peeing incident, make sure you are at
least 200 feet away from water sources. Drip-drying requires no TP at
all; all-natural TP is preferable to paper because paper needs to be
carried out.

Bathing

Things that we often do at least once a day in our regular sanitary
existence—putting on clean clothes, taking a shower, washing our
hair—are all optional in the backcountry. (These could also be more
optional at home; see the Conclusion: Adopting an LNT Lifestyle.)
When it comes to minimizing human impact in our precious wildlands, the less you use soap, the better.

The only practice that should not be considered optional is regularly washing your hands—especially after visiting a cat hole or before preparing a meal. In fact, you can go for two weeks without washing your hair and it will not impact a soul, but failure to wash your hands just once could pass a parasite that makes everyone in camp sick.

As with all washing activities, clean your hands at least 200 feet away from water sources. Carry a bottle of water or (ideally) a pot of warm water away from the water source, preferably to a durable surface such as gravel or slickrock. Wet your hands, use a small amount of phosphate-free, biodegradable soap, lather up, and rinse by pouring water over your hands, not by dipping your hands into the pot of water. Avoid any contamination of soap on cooking utensils, or the soap can give you diarrhea. If you choose to wash your hair or bathe, this same method should be used. Bathing in a large lake, stream, or river is acceptable, by LNT standards, if you *do not* use soap. And if you swim in your clothes, you can wash them (without soap) at the same time.

LNT Basics: Backcountry Hygiene

Health Precautions

- Boil or filter and treat water before drinking it.
- Wash your hands after pooping and/or peeing, and before preparing food.

Human Waste

- If there is an outhouse provided, use it, to concentrate impact.
- In most backcountry situations where there is no outhouse, burying your waste in a shallow cat hole is the best disposal method.
- The cat hole should be located at least 200 feet from any water sources, campsites, and trails.
- Maximum conditions for decomposition are achieved when the hole is dug in organic soil (rich in microorganisms) and in a spot that is somewhat moist but receives a fair amount of sunlight.

- Use a trowel to dig a hole that is about 4 to 8 inches deep, and 4 to 6 inches in diameter.
- Once you have made a deposit, throw in some soil and stir the stuff with a stick. Then place at least 2 inches of topsoil back in the hole and camouflage the site.
- Dig a latrine if you are camping in a large group that is staying at the same site several nights or that contains young children who are not capable of digging a cat hole.
- Pack out all toilet paper, or avoid the hassle by using a natural wiping alternative such as snow, leaves, or river stones.
- Tampons and disposable diapers must be packed out as well.
- Avoid urinating on plants because animals are attracted to the salty liquid.

Bathing

- With the exception of hand washing, bathing should be considered optional in the backcountry because it has inevitable environmental impacts.
- Any washing activities should take place at least 200 feet from natural water sources and, preferably, on a durable surface such as gravel or slickrock.
- If you use soap, make sure it is phosphate free and biodegradable.
- If you do not use soap, washing in a natural body of water is acceptable by LNT standards only if it is a large lake or river.
- Minimize tooth-brushing impact by using salt or baking soda instead of toothpaste.

It is unrealistic to expect to feel squeaky-clean when visiting the backcountry. However, everyone has to find their own hygienic comfort level and determine what practices they can and cannot give up. I know one person who is the most rugged of wilderness travelers in every respect, except for the fact that he becomes grumpy if he does not wash his hair every day. Whereas I have got to put on clean underwear and brush my teeth every morning. (You can minimize the impact of oral hygiene by using salt or baking soda instead of toothpaste; spray spit through your teeth, or swallow it unless it contains fluoride.) But for some NOLS field instructors, many forms of washing—except for the hands—go out the window when they are out in the backcountry on courses that often last a month.

"We spent thirty-six showerless days on Denali one time and finally caught one of the park's shuttle buses for a ride back to civilization," recalled NOLS instructor and LNT pioneer Drew Leemon in recent correspondence. "We did not notice our aroma, but the other visitors did. They would wave the bus over for a lift, climb partway onboard, wrinkle their noses, and decide to wait for the next shuttle."

Such spartan hygiene practices may seem extreme to folks who have rarely gone a day without showering, but longtime NOLS staffers say minimal bathing in the backcountry has its benefits. "Thirty days of dirt makes your hair softer and smoother when you wash it," observed Marit Sawyer in recent correspondence. "And a good wet-sand scrub, followed by a plunge in an icy lake, feels better than any commercial mud, apricot, or avocado skin treatment."

CHAPTER 3

THE WILDERNESS ON FOOT

LNT Guidelines for Hikers, Climbers, and Backcountry Skiers

WHEN I BACKPACK THROUGH WILDERNESS areas in southern Utah, I always feel a certain kinship with the Anasazi Indians who traveled through the same canyons hundreds of years before me. They, like me, were walkers. They did not have horses or the wheel for locomotion— they relied on their arms and legs to get them everywhere they needed to go.

An intricate system of ancient paths throughout the Southwest's Four Corners region testifies to the long distances the Anasazi traveled on foot. Ladders comprised of handholds and footholds carved into sheer rock below the ruins of Anasazi cliff dwellings proves they were skilled climbers. And artifacts resembling snowshoes indicate these people kept walking in winter.

Hiking, climbing, snowshoeing and skiing are quiet and simple forms of foot-propelled travel. Unfortunately, many backcountry pathways are now crowded with hikers, popular cliff faces are crawling with climbers, and once-remote winter wonderlands are congested with backcountry skiers. The growing number of people enjoying these very basic outdoor pursuits is causing a variety of environmental complications.

If we are to preserve our wildlands for future generations, it is just as important for a solo hiker to take precautions to minimize his or her impact on the land as it is for a large horse packing party. What follows is a look at some of the particular environmental and social concerns that come with hiking, climbing, and backcountry skiing, and a guide to specific LNT techniques that will help you minimize your impact.

▲ ▲ ▲

To Hike or Not to Hike with Rover

Although pets are banned from most national park trails, it is common to see people traveling and camping with their dogs in most other wildland areas. For the dog, roaming about in the backcountry is a great thrill and beats a boring city park any day. However, bringing these domestic animals into a wild area often disturbs other users and it has a negative impact on the environment. Dogs chase other people's dogs, they harass wildlife (which can have serious consequences with a threatened species like bighorn sheep), they bark, they disrupt water sources, and they defecate on the trail and at campsites.

But with all this being said, some people (women backpacking alone, for instance) find that a well-trained dog is a faithful trail companion and is worth taking the extra precautions to minimize the animal's impact on the environment. If after weighing the pros and cons, you decide to take your dog with you into the backcountry, follow these guidelines to keep your dog and its inevitable impacts in check:

- Try to choose a rarely visited destination where there will be little chance of contact with other users.
- Regardless of where you are, keep your dog on the trail and restrained from chasing wildlife.
- Restrain your dog from barking at and jumping up on other hikers.
- When your furry friend leaves a little doggie pile, pull out your trowel and bury it away from the trail and water

sources in a cat hole just as you would human feces.
- Instead of allowing your dog to romp through springs and ponds—which will likely scare away area wildlife from a critical water source for some time—scoop the water into a bowl and let Fido lap it up 200 feet away.
- Prevent your dog from defecating in water. Dogs, like beavers and other animals, can carry *Giardia* and thus can contaminate water.
- In camp, keep your dog restrained or have it trained to stay within the site; a wandering dog will disturb wildlife and perhaps other campers.
- Dog food is very aromatic and will attract wildlife. Secure it with your own food.
- Keep your dog from barking.

HIKING: LIFE IN THE TRENCHES

Merely walking through the wilderness seems innocuous enough. However, it is by far the most common mode of recreational travel, and all those little footprints can combine to create a big environmental mess. In fact, increased trail use from hikers has prompted most land managers to cite erosion and plant damage caused by human trampling as the number one trail problem in wilderness areas.

Such destruction is not completely the hikers' fault. Many paths in national parks and Forest Service wilderness areas are old game trails or routes blazed by frontier settlers more than a century ago. These trails are often poorly constructed and placed in less than optimal locations that promote, rather than help prevent, user-caused erosion. In Great Smoky Mountains National Park, for example, most of the 930 miles of official park trails follow historic settler wagon roads or old railroad grades that were built for hauling timber.

"The wagon roads vary in design, often crisscrossing streams, ascending ridges, and showing evidence of severe erosion long before their use as trails," noted a 1994 study of trail conditions in the park by John Wilson and Joseph Seney. Not surprisingly, the study found that a high level of visitor traffic on park trails, combined with poor trail

A researcher studies trampling impacts caused by hiking. (photo by David Cole)

construction, made the environmental condition of these paths, in most cases, downright unsightly. "Trail widening around muddy sections in excess of 12 feet is not uncommon," noted the study.

Minimizing Trail Erosion

In a perfect world, the trail maintenance budget for Great Smoky Mountains National Park and other public lands would be adequate for land managers to reroute poorly located trails and maintain deteriorating paths. However, this is rarely the case because most federal land management agency budgets are of dismal proportions and if any trail maintenance is performed at all, it is done by volunteer groups. Consequently, the best way to keep bad trails from getting worse is for hikers to walk softly and smartly, and, basically, abide by the Leave No Trace principle of "travel on durable surfaces."

What is durable? Is it best to travel on existing trails or hike cross-country? The answer to these questions can vary dramatically depending on your geographic location, and the type of area—a crowded state park or a remote Alaskan wilderness, for example—that you are visiting. Just like choosing a campsite, deciding when and where to leave your bootprints is a judgment call that should be based on your consideration of pertinent environmental factors and minimum-impact hiking techniques.

- First, find out about any hiking or trail restrictions that have been imposed by the local land manager. If you are visiting a location where use is high and off-trail trampling is a big problem, like the White Mountains in New Hampshire or Phoenix Mountain Preserve in Arizona, policies may require you to stay on established trails, and wandering cross-country could be illegal.
- In places that receive a fair to heavy amount of use, it is usually best to concentrate impact and stick to designated trails. Traveling cross-country may give you more privacy or improve the aesthetics of your backpacking experience, but where your boots tread, others will surely follow. In some environments, like a forested understory, it only takes a few people passing on the same route to trample sensitive plants to death and create a discernible path where there once was none.
- When hiking on existing trails, make sure you are following the designated main trail and not "volunteer" trails that are often created by people trying to avoid mud or shortcut up switchbacks.
- Wear gaiters and walk through the mud rather than contributing to the widening of the trail by tiptoeing around the muck in an effort to keep your feet clean.
- If you are traveling on fairly flat, dry terrain and your pack is not

too heavy, consider wearing lightweight hiking boots instead of the heavy, lug-soled variety. Although studies on how different kinds of hiking boot treads impact trail erosion have proven inconclusive, there is no reason to pummel mild terrain with the tread equivalent of a tractor tire.

- Other ways to minimize trail erosion include walking single file and avoiding locations altogether that you know are especially muddy after a rain or during spring snowmelt.

Cross-country Travel

When you are visiting more remote backcountry areas where established trails are few and far between, and durable surfaces exist for travel routes, hiking cross-country may well be a responsible minimum-impact choice. When you get right down to it, trails themselves are a kind of impact and, on a philosophical level, they are contradictory to the mandate of the Wilderness Act to keep designated lands free of signs of humans.

But on a practical level, being able to travel cross-country without impacting the land, and not leaving a path that will invite others to impact it behind you, is a very difficult thing to do. Sticking to a designated trail is much easier than constantly weighing the environmental pros and cons that come with choosing a cross-country route.

If you choose to hike cross-country, or find yourself in a situation where you have no other choice, keep in mind the following:

- The most durable surfaces for cross-country travel are gravel, sand, slickrock, snow, dry alpine meadows and grasslands, and deep duff beneath a dense forest overstory.
- Avoid striking out on a vegetated forest floor or on soggy meadows and grasslands—this terrain is far less resistant to trampling.
- Some special types of soils, such as cryptobiotic crusts in desert environments (see Desert Travel in chapter 6, Special Environments), should be diligently avoided because a single bootprint will last for years.
- Hiking across a trail-less landscape can be an exhilarating experience, but not if you get lost. Before heading out, make sure you have the proper topographical map for the area and know how to read it.

- Never compensate for your lack of orienteering skills by scarring the land to mark your route with signs like tree blazes or cairns.
- Avoid traversing steep slopes; heel marks gouged into the soil will invariably cause erosion.
- Unlike hiking on a trail, the best way for a group to minimize the impact of their cross-country travel is to spread out across the landscape rather than walking single file.

When traveling cross country where there is no trail, spread out to mitigate trampling impacts. (photo courtesy of NOLS)

Avoiding Conflicts with Other Users

It is important to be realistic about what you can expect when visiting a certain backcountry location. Finding solitude is no longer something that can be taken for granted in wilderness areas—especially those that are located within a few hours' drive of major cities. If solitude and/or avoiding horse packing parties or mountain bike riders is a top priority, research ahead of time the trail you plan to hike and find out from a knowledgeable land manager what kind of traffic that area receives.

- In the event you encounter a party of horseback riders, the courteous thing to do—because pack animals can sometimes be spooked—is to pull off on the downhill side of the trail until the group passes.
- If you encounter a mountain biker who does not yield or is in an area off-limits to fat tires, politely inform him or her of the offense; perhaps the behavior is the result of ignorance or can be changed with a little positive peer pressure.

LNT Basics: Hiking

Minimize Trail Erosion

- Hike on established trails whenever possible and stay off unofficial "volunteer" trails.
- Walk through the mud rather than around it; wear gaiters if you want to keep the dirt out of your boots.
- Groups should hike single file.
- On flat, dry terrain consider wearing lightweight boots or tennis shoes rather than heavy lug soles.
- Avoid visiting especially muddy areas after a heavy rain or during spring snowmelt.

Cross-country Travel

Cross-country travel should generally be avoided, but if you end up hiking off trail make sure you do the following:

- Hike on durable surfaces like gravel, sand, slickrock, snow, dry alpine meadows and grasslands, and deep duff beneath a dense forest overstory.

- Some special types of soils, such as cryptobiotic crusts in desert environments, should be diligently avoided because a single bootprint will last for years.
- Before heading out, make sure you have the proper topographical map for the area and you know how to read it. Getting lost is bad for you and the environment.
- If you are in a group, spread out across the landscape rather than walking single file.

Social and Environmental Considerations

- Adhere to area or route closures, whether for bird nesting, archaeological, or other reasons.
- If you encounter a party of horseback riders, pull off on the downhill side of the trail until the group passes.
- Solitude is getting harder and harder to find. Consult a land manager before heading out if you are hoping to visit a place with plenty of peace and quiet.

CLIMBING: EVERYONE WANTS A PIECE OF THE ROCK

Sally Moser considers herself a "traditional climber"—one who cut her teeth on routes in remote backcountry rather than in a climbing gym. She got involved in the sport some twenty years ago, spending her days scaling the mountainsides in Yosemite and other Western wilderness areas. "It was just a few of us out on the rock then," she recalled in a recent conversation. "Now there are hundreds of thousands of climbers out there. And with so many of us, we cannot just go climb anywhere like we used to. We have to think about impact."

The traditional climbers like Moser say many of these new converts lack the environmental ethic and appreciation for being in the great outdoors that is shared by the old-timers. "These people have learned to climb in the gym and they are not out there to enjoy the place—they are rad and cool, and want to be seen by other climbers doing a difficult route," said Moser.

Mark Magnuson, a ranger at Grand Teton National Park and a Leave No Trace master, agreed in an LNT newsletter article. "Most climbers used to come from a tradition of hiking, camping, and

Big wall climbers in Zion National Park (photo by Chris Gould)

outdoorsmanship," he wrote. "Somewhere along the line, the climbing community lost its land ethic."

Although many new climbers who consider themselves environmentally sensitive would likely take issue with Magnuson's assessment, few can dispute the fact that—attitudes aside—just the sheer number of people recently drawn to the sport is causing many popular climbing areas to be trashed. A proliferation of unnecessary trails to routes,

Look for trail signs marking an established trail to a climbing area (photo courtesy The Access Fund)

campfire scars, litter, and toilet paper flowers are among the preventable human impacts frequently encountered in once pristine spots. At the very least, these impacts take away from the outdoor experience of other users; at the very worst—from a climber's perspective—land managers close the area to climbing in an effort to protect the resource.

Indeed, El Capitan in Yosemite has experienced so much impact from climbers that the accumulation of human waste in some places on the mountain has created what Moser describes as "open sewers." To cope with the waste problem, park managers now require climbers on the more popular big walls to pack out their poop. It is one of many new regulations and controversies that have popped up as a result of the hordes of people who are now drawn to what was once an obscure sport.

In addition to being a traditional climber, Moser is also executive director of The Access Fund. The nonprofit organization works to keep climbing areas open and promote environmental conservation of those areas. "We are trying to get the minimum-impact message out to climbers—especially to all the newcomers to the sport," said Moser. "We want to educate them on Leave No Trace practices, and help them make better environmental decisions when they are out there."

Environmentally responsible climbing boils down to putting the resource first rather than the route. This means you should consider how your behavior in a climbing area—from throwing down a cigarette butt to driving a bolt in the rock—impacts the environmental integrity of the landscape. Obviously, there are no such concerns in a climbing gym, but there is also no replacement for the real thing. Climbers who are not willing to give the land the respect it deserves should stay at the gym.

Taking the Best Approach

Leave No Trace climbing begins with the approach. Instead of making a beeline through the brush to get to the base of the climb, spend a few minutes to find an established trail. Concentrating traffic on one primary trail helps protect vegetation in the area and keeps soils from being trampled by a multitude of carelessly created footpaths.

If you are setting up camp near the base, try to locate an established site, and follow the minimum-impact guidelines detailed in chapters 1, All About Camping, and 2, LNT Principles of Hygiene and the Wilderness Bathroom.

Responsible Waste Disposal

Take extra care in camp and when climbing to pack out all your trash—and that left by others before you. Small pieces of litter, like cigarette butts or apple cores, add up in popular climbing areas. Plus, food scraps of any kind attract animals and disrupt their natural feeding habits. Consider taking a trash bag with you up the crag to help pick up all the crud that less-conscientious climbers leave behind.

Proper disposal of human waste is becoming an increasingly problematic issue as more and more climbers are drawn to rock. One of the most common contributions The Access Fund makes to climbing areas is to pay for the installation of vault toilets near popular crags. If you are climbing where there is a toilet, use it for all your evacuation needs.

In the absence of a toilet, climbers (like backpackers) usually do not have a lot of good options these days for LNT-approved poop placement. If you happen to be in a spot where there is a lot of fairly deep organic soil around, you can dig a cat hole; or if you are in a very remote alpine area above tree line, smearing the stuff on a rock may be the way to go. However, considering the growing visitor traffic in most climbing areas, it is increasingly unlikely that either of these situations will exist, and packing out your poop will be the best evacuation technique.

It once was accepted practice for big wall climbers and climbers ascending multiple-day routes to make deposits in paper bags and toss them over the side. However, this is now against land management regulations in many places, including Yosemite and Zion National Parks, and it is an environmentally and socially irresponsible option just about anywhere you toss it. Today the preferred method of packing it out for wall climbers is the poop tube—a homemade PVC pipe contraption that hangs neatly from the bottom of the climber's haul sack (for details on how to build your own, see Sea Kayaking in chapter 5, Minimizing Impacts on Waterways).

Considering Others

When climbing, choose a route that will not disturb wildlife or archaeological sites. Pay attention to where birds, especially owls, falcons, eagles, hawks, and other raptors, circle and land on cliff faces and bluffs. If it appears the bird may have a nest near where you are planning to climb, choose another route. Birds can be easily

Try to make sure your chosen climbing route is in an area where you won't disturb raptors. (photo by Chris Gould)

stressed by humans approaching their nests, especially during spring and early summer.

In the event that you inadvertently encounter a nest on a climb, never touch it; human contact may cause the adults to abandon the nest and its eggs or young. Land managers in parks and wilderness areas often impose seasonal closures at climbing areas to protect nesting sites. Respect these temporary regulations and find another place to climb.

Likewise, many excellent climbing routes, especially in the Southwest, are located near ancient Native American archaeological sites. Avoid touching or disturbing rock art and ruins, and respect land management restrictions imposed to protect these resources. (For more information on how to minimize impact around archaeological and historical sites, see chapter 6, Special Environments.)

Also, be aware of social impacts at climbing areas; the desired atmosphere at outdoor destinations is often quite different for most people from that typically found at a gym. Loud boom boxes, barking and/or unleashed dogs, and climbers monopolizing routes can ruin the experience of other climbers trying to enjoy the area. In popular climbing areas where you are sharing the spot with others, it is best to leave the boom box and dog at home.

Protecting the Rock

Finally, climbers should do as much as possible to minimize the direct impact the sport has on the rock, without compromising their personal safety. For instance:

Protection: Use removable protection and natural anchors wherever possible; placing bolts and pitons scars the rock and can detract from a climbing area's natural beauty.

Prior to 1970, it was a common practice for climbers to ascend a route by hammering pitons into the rock, which inevitably damaged the resource and caused land managers to close areas to climbers in some popular places. Equipment manufacturers responded to the problem by developing devices known as removable protection—aluminum wedges, cams, and spring-loaded camming devices that can be placed and then removed from a route without damaging the rock.

Relying on removable protection to ascend a route, called "clean climbing," has been standard practice among environmentally conscious climbers for nearly three decades and is clearly the best way to "leave no trace" on the rock.

Chalk: Minimize your use of chalk. Like fixed anchors, chalk leaves marks on the rock—albeit less permanent—that others see, and it detracts from the natural character of the landscape. The best way to do this is with a sock or ball to reduce the amount of chalk on your hands.

The sock method involves taking an old sock, putting chalk in it and tying it off, and then placing it in your chalk bag. The ball is a commercial version of the sock concept. Either way, you get just a little bit of chalk on your hands, which means less on the rock—and some climbers claim the minimal chalk approach even gives you a better grip.

Scrubbing: Avoid disturbing the rock to make a route more comfortable. The process of scrubbing—also known as gardening—should be carried out with great discretion on a new route, and vegetation should only be disturbed for safety reasons rather than aesthetic ones.

Bolting: Follow the practices established by the agency that oversees the climbing site. You can minimize the visual impact of the bolt by using camouflaged bolt hangers and camouflaged webbing for the rappel anchor, and by placing the bolt in a spot that is not so obvious from the ground.

Descending: Once you have completed the ascent, getting down raises another impact issue—rappeling versus walking off. Good LNT judgment is key here. If hiking down is possible, if the area has an established trail you can use, and if the trail is not suffering from trampling impacts, walking off may be the best option. However, if you are in a popular area and trampling is a problem (or walking off just is not possible), rappeling will likely be the way to go.

LNT Basics: Climbing

Approach
- Follow established trails when approaching a route.
- When camping at the base of the climb, try to stay at established campsites.
- Pack out all trash in camp and on the climbing route (bring a trash bag to pick up the litter of others).

Waste Disposal
- Use an outhouse whenever it is available.
- Dig a cat hole if there is enough soil in the area where you are climbing.
- In the absence of an outhouse or diggable soil, pack out

your poop in a PVC pipe or other device (never toss it off the mountain).

Social and Environmental Considerations

- Adhere to area or route closures, whether for bird nesting, archaeological, or other reasons.
- Avoid climbing near bird nests and archaeological sites.
- In popular climbing areas where you are sharing the spot with others, it is probably best to leave the boom box and dog at home.

Minimize Impacts on the Rock

- Use removable protection and natural anchors wherever possible.
- Exercise good judgment when deciding how to get down. Use either an established rappel station or an established descent route (if using the path will not obviously contribute to its deterioration).
- Try to use as little chalk as possible.
- The process of scrubbing—also known as gardening— should be carried out with great discretion on a new route, and vegetation should only be disturbed for safety reasons rather than aesthetic ones.

CROSS-COUNTRY SKIING: PROTECTING THE WINTER WONDERLAND

Venturing into the backcountry for a camping trip during the dead of winter, when the ground is covered with deep snow and temperatures dip below zero, used to be the pastime of a few warm-blooded souls. National parks like Yellowstone, which have bumper-to-bumper traffic in the summer, would be completely devoid of people. But today, with the advent of high-tech, cold-weather gear and people's increasing desire to experience wilderness settings in solitude, backcountry skiing and winter camping is becoming a popular pursuit. In fact, cross-country skiing is one of the fastest-growing outdoor sports in the United States.

In national parks, for example, winter visitation has increased 27 percent in the last decade; summer visitation has increased only

7 percent. The Yellowstone backcountry is now getting so many visitors during winter that park managers are considering imposing restrictions to handle human impacts.

The good thing about backcountry skiing and winter camping is that some of the biggest impact problems during other times of year—like trampling of trails and campsites—are, essentially, nonexistent when the ground is covered with a thick blanket of snow. However, the potential for stressing wildlife is significantly greater during winter and is the biggest LNT challenge.

Snow Camping

Even though the nights are cold and long, try to resist the urge to have a campfire. During winter, when all downed wood is buried under the snow and the only available fuel is tree branches, fires are a bad idea. As a "warm-glow" alternative, bring plenty of fuel for your stove and try candle lanterns.

Upon leaving camp, dismantle your snow shelter and fluff up the white stuff so that visitors coming after you can enjoy a more natural setting.

When snow-camping, avoid building a fire; use your stove and good clothing for warmth. (photo by Chris Gould)

Winter Waste Disposal

The only good option for waste disposal in snow-covered environs is to pack it out (refer to the methods described in the climbing section of this chapter); burying your poop in the snow is pointless because it will just stay frozen until spring and then it will reappear in full form. When you pee, be sure to do it away from ski trails, and cover up the yellow snow so others do not have to look at it.

LNT Basics: Cross-country Skiing

Watch Out for Wildlife

- When traveling through the backcountry, never approach wildlife; try to stick to established ski trails so that human activity is contained in a specific area.
- Take extra care to avoid locating your camp where there is animal sign indicating that it is a spot where wildlife feed, water, or sleep.

Waste Disposal

- Pack out your poop.
- When you pee, do it away from trails.

Snow Camping

- Resist the urge to have a campfire when deep snow prevents you from reaching downed wood.
- Upon leaving camp, dismantle your snow shelter and fluff up the white stuff so that visitors coming after you can enjoy a more natural setting.

Watching Out for Wildlife

In snowy climates, winter is the toughest time of year for mammals that do not hibernate. As food becomes more difficult to find, the animals have less energy and they must conserve every last ounce to help them find their next meal. When a deer or elk, for example, sees a skier approaching, its natural instinct is to flee, which elevates its heart rate and uses up valuable energy reserves. For a healthy animal during a normal winter, this may not cause serious problems, but if the winter is particularly harsh and the snow is deep, the added stress of humans could be fatal.

When traveling through the backcountry, never approach wildlife, and try to stick to established ski trails so that human activity is contained in a specific area. Although there is plenty of research confirming that humans stress wildlife in winter, there is no set distance that has been established as an adequate buffer zone between you and the animal; several hundred yards should be enough. Also, take extra care to avoid locating your camp where there is animal sign (which is easy to see in the snow) that indicates that it is a spot where wildlife feed, water, or sleep.

CHAPTER 4

RIDING SOFTLY IN THE SADDLE

LNT Guidelines for Mountain Bikers and Equestrians

ASK ANY LAND MANAGER WHAT is the most common gripe he or she hears from backcountry users and it will probably either be about unruly mountain bikers or obnoxious horse packers. In terms of sheer numbers, there are likely far more unruly and/or obnoxious hikers in many backcountry areas, because hikers comprise the largest wildland user group. But there is something about those horses and bicycles that really gets under people's skin—when they are not the ones sitting in the saddle, of course.

A 1994 survey by John Wilson and Joseph Seney of hiker-biker relations in the popular Rattlesnake National Recreation Area (NRA), located on the outskirts of Missoula, Montana, showed that nearly two-thirds of the hikers found mountain bikes on area trails "objectionable." The two most common reasons given by hikers were "too many bicycles" and "bicycles traveling too fast."

The user-conflict situation for hikers and horse packers is not much better. In Montana's Bob Marshall Wilderness Complex, for example, horse use increased 20 percent between 1970 and 1983. During that same period, the number of hikers entering the wilderness nearly doubled. The result of this significant increase in wilderness use— albeit primarily from hikers—was a barrage of complaints to land managers about negative impacts of pack stock in the Bob Marshall. Hikers objected to having to walk through too much horse crap, and complained of environmental destruction to trails, campsites, and riparian areas caused by the proliferation of the large beasts.

As in almost all research conducted on user conflicts, both the Rattlesnake NRA and Bob Marshall Wilderness studies (the latter by Cole and McClaran) showed that the "conflict relationship" between the differing parties was "asymmetrical." That is, while the hikers were generally annoyed by the mountain bikers and horse packers, only a few bikers or equestrians reported having their visitor experience negatively impacted by hikers.

Whether mountain bikes or horses actually cause more environmental damage to a wildland destination than hikers varies dramatically from place to place, depending on the type of terrain and behavior of the various user groups. There is no denying, however, that fat tire tracks and hoofprints leave a very recognizable impact on the land— especially if it is in a place that is receiving more than its fair share of human visitors.

History has borne out that when user conflicts and/or environmental impacts become too great in a particular backcountry area, land managers often close trails to mountain bikers and pack stock. Regardless of whether this is deserved in any particular situation is beside the point. The real prospect that tracts of public land can be made off-limits to biking or horseback riding even for perceived environmental impacts should be motivation enough to adopt Leave No Trace practices. But, even more important, it is the responsibility of all users— including mountain bikers and equestrians—to do their share in preserving the landscape and sense of solitude that makes wildlands so special. To that end, here are some specific LNT guidelines and minimum-impact techniques for you to ride by.

▲ ▲ ▲

The Multiple-use Solution

The history of the world is shaped by turf battles. For as long as anyone can remember, people of different cultures, religions, and agendas have been refusing to share their territory and, instead, duking it out.

Among such ongoing disputes are the conflicts between different recreational user groups visiting our nation's public lands. It may seem like a minuscule concern when compared to other conflicts currently raging around the planet, but the inability of various types of people to get along when trying to have fun in the backcountry is the source of major headaches for land managers.

Hostilities between mountain bikers and hikers in northern California escalated to the point in the late 1980s where there were biker-hiker clashes in which bones were broken and some anti-biking vigilantes booby-trapped trails with fishing line to stop (and injure) speeding members of the knobby tire set. However, that is about the extent of the violence in user conflicts; usually these encounters result in nothing more than heated verbal exchanges and complaints to land managers.

The real danger that comes from this ill will between the many different people visiting the backcountry for different reasons is that it undermines environmental protection of our public lands. While larger threats loom—like irresponsible logging of our national forests and commercial development in and around parks—land managers are distracted by never-ending conflicts between hikers, horseback riders, and mountain bikers. Plus, if these three substantial user groups were to comprise a unified rather than a divided front, it would be a conservation force to be reckoned with—large enough to shape management decisions and protect our public lands from being eaten away by consumptive uses like logging, mining, grazing, and development.

So why do we nonmotorized recreationists not get along in the backcountry? Part of the problem lies in the same reason why people are rude to each other on the New York City subway—it is too crowded. This is not the case everywhere, but most people go to the same places, to the most accessible Forest Service lands and the most popular national parks. A large majority of the 830 million recreation visits to national forest lands in 1995 occurred in a limited number of wilderness areas and other popular destinations that are within a few hours' drive of metropolitan areas.

"Trails in or near cities tend to be crowded, and crowded trails breed user conflict," said Tim Blumenthal, executive director of the International Mountain Biking Association, in a recent conversation. "The key factor is more people. There is a gap between expectations and reality. The farther you are from a population center, the more likely it is that you expect solitude. And as we all know, solitude is getting tougher to find."

Considering our differences, and the inevitable prospect that recreational use of public lands will continue to increase in the coming years, can we nonmotorized folks ever expect to all get along? The answer to this dilemma in most places across the country is that we have no choice. At best, the amount of public lands available for recreational pursuits will generally stay the same; this means more hikers, mountain bikers, and horseback riders will be vying for trail space, and the potential for user conflicts will be even greater.

Sometimes land managers consider segregating trail users—putting, for example, horseback riders on one path or detour route and directing hikers to another route—but this is a counterproductive move from an environmental standpoint, because it spreads human impact over a larger region. Closing trails to certain users, such as mountain bikers, is often counterproductive as well because it denies access to a large and growing trail constituency group.

In most cases the best solution is to manage trails as

"multiple use" (open to hikers, horseback riders, and mountain bikers in nonwilderness areas, and open to hikers and horseback riders in wilderness areas), and to rely on users to educate one another on the principles of Leave No Trace and basic multiple-use manners.

Whether it is deciding to split a large—and potentailly loud—party into smaller camping groups or yielding right of way on the trail, practicing good multiple-use manners boils down simply to being considerate and keeping in mind the big conservation picture. Most of the nation's newest long-distance paths, such as the American Discovery Trail, the Continental Divide Trail, and the Arizona Trail, are designed, at least in part, to be shared by hikers, horseback riders, and mountain bikers.

The multiple-use approach is working; right of way for the trails is easier to obtain from land managers because there is a broader base of user support, and, likewise, there is also a larger community of trail users to help maintain and protect the nonmotorized path when it is completed. Plus, from a conservation standpoint, a nonmotorized trails constituency that is unified is far more effective in fighting larger, more political environmental threats such as proposals to allow clear-cutting near the trail or strip mining or opening the path to off-road vehicle use. If backcountry recreationists are going to engage in a turf war, it might as well be a battle worth fighting.

MOUNTAIN BIKING: AS THE FAT TIRE TURNS

Back in 1964 when Congress passed the Wilderness Act, the only two modes of nonmotorized travel on public lands was either by foot or horse. Few could have anticipated that twenty years later millions of people would be vying for space on trails atop all-terrain knobby-tire bicycles. Ownership of mountain bikes in the United States has exploded over the last several decades from essentially zero in the late 1970s when the fat tire machine was invented to some 26 million today. Many of these bike owners stick to city sidewalks and rural roads, but millions have become dedicated backcountry trail riders as well. It is the rapid onslaught of this new user group that has, perhaps, impacted the experiences of all wildland recreationists more than any other recent public lands development.

Learning Social Graces

The impact problems associated with mountain biking in the backcountry are as much—or more—social than environmental. Hikers and horseback riders do not like the feeling of almost being mowed down by a group of speeding mountain bikers. Even when there are no mountain bikers in sight, their tracks on the trail are easily recognizable and, for many other users, instantly despicable. For land managers, there is often nothing more irritating than seeing the telltale fat tire tracks on wilderness trails where mountain bikes are off-limits.

"We have to overcome a stereotype," said International Mountain Biking Association (IMBA) executive director Tim Blumenthal in a recent conversation about mountain biking's reputation as an environmentally insensitive gonzo sport. "It is not just the gonzo riders anymore; a broad range of people are getting into off-road mountain biking these days." However, Blumenthal also pointed out that one gonzo rider blasting past forty people on a trail over the course of a day can do a lot to perpetuate mountain biking's bad-boy image. "A mountain biker breaking the rules of the trail is very noticeable," he noted. "But if a hiker were to take off cross-country up a hill rather than going up the switchbacks, few other people would probably see it."

Formed in 1988 in response to the increasing number of trails that were being closed to fat tires, IMBA works with land managers and the public to protect public land access for mountain bikes, and to teach this new user group some manners. Although IMBA can count many success stories in securing access for mountain bikers, Blumenthal acknowledged that several big problems still exist for the future of fat tire trail travel. "We have not been around long enough or presented ourselves well enough to command widespread respect." And, he continued, "We have to figure a way to corral unruly riders who ignore trail signs and hammer on busy routes."

Blumenthal maintains that mountain biking is not any more damaging to trails and the environment than foot traffic. A variety of studies on the subject have concluded as much, including the report released
in 1994 by Wilson and Seney that evaluated erosional impacts of mountain trails in Montana. This particular study found that horse traffic
had the greatest potential for erosion, followed by hiking traffic, with
the fat tire stirring up the least amount of trail soil. However, the report also noted that the findings of the study were "complicated and
difficult to decipher."

While research has generally been inconclusive in proving the
extent to which mountain-bike use negatively impacts the environment, there is no shortage of data documenting how much most hikers
dislike sharing the trail with mountain bikers. The survey of hiker-
biker relations in Montana's Rattlesnake National Recreation Area that
showed nearly two-thirds of the hikers found mountain bikes on area
trails "objectionable" also noted that, while both hikers and bikers ex-
pressed a strong degree of attachment to the area, "bicyclists reported
significantly less focus on the setting than the other groups."

But regardless of how they are interpreted, such findings are no
license for mountain bikers to be any less conscientious about minimizing their environmental impact. "Tracks in the mud are easy to trace
back to bicycles," noted Blumenthal. "Heavy use is going to impact
trails no matter what—whether it is coming from bikes or hikers or
horses. But mountain bikers have a special responsibility to minimize
their impact. And IMBA is adamant about riders staying on the trail."

Salvation through Soft Cycling

To that end, IMBA and other environmentally conscious mountain
biking groups encourage a kind of non-gonzo approach to riding that
has been referred to as "soft cycling." (To contact IMBA, see the appendix.) Among the key commandments of this politically correct form
of pedaling are:
- Stay off muddy trails.
- Avoid heavy braking.
- Walk your bike over a trail obstruction rather than cutting a "line"
  around it.

Mountain bikers should always ride on designated trails. (photo by Chris Gould)

- Stay on switchbacks.
- Ride single file and in small groups.
- Slow down—especially around other trail users.

IMBA has incorporated this general "soft cycling" philosophy into its more specific "Rules of the Trail." Like the six principles of the Leave No Trace program, these six rules are heavily promoted by IMBA and various mountain bike manufacturers that have printed the guidelines on water bottles and product hang-tags. The six IMBA rules to ride by are:

Ride on open trails only: Respect trail and road closures; avoid possible trespass on private land. Federal and state wilderness areas are closed to cycling.

Leave no trace: Be sensitive to the dirt beneath you. Even on open trails, do not ride under conditions in which you will leave evidence of your passing, such as on damp or muddy soils shortly after a rain. This also means staying on the trail and not creating any new ones. Pack out what you pack in.

Control your bicycle: Inattention for even a second can cause problems. Obey all speed laws.

Always yield on the trail: Make known your approach well in advance. Show your respect when passing others by slowing to a walk or even stopping. Anticipate that other trail users may be around corners or in blind spots.

Never spook animals: All animals are startled by an unannounced approach. Give animals extra room and time to adjust to you. In passing, use special care and follow directions of horseback riders (ask if uncertain).

Plan ahead: Know your equipment, your ability, and the area in which you are riding—and prepare accordingly. A well-executed trip is a satisfaction to you and not a burden or offense to others.

When it comes to minimizing fat tire impacts and improving the image of mountain biking, Blumenthal pointed out that it is not just about what you do when you are riding. "We encourage mountain bikers to join a local club, to get involved in volunteer trail work, and to participate in National Trails Day (held every June)," he said.

LNT Basics: Mountain Biking

Soft Cycling Principles
- Stay off muddy trails.
- Avoid heavy braking.
- Walk your bike over a trail obstruction rather than cutting a "line" around it.

- Stay on switchbacks.
- Ride single file and in small groups.
- Slow down—especially around other trail users.

Rules of the Trail
- **Ride on open trails only:** Respect trail and road closures; avoid possible trespass on private land.
- **Leave no trace:** Even on open trails, do not ride under conditions in which you will leave evidence of your passing, such as on certain soils shortly after a rain. This also means staying on the trail and not creating any new ones. Pack out what you pack in.
- **Control your bicycle:** Inattention for even a second can cause problems.
- **Always yield the trail:** Make known your approach well in advance. When passing others, slow to a walk or even stop. Anticipate that other trail users may be around corners or in blind spots.
- **Never spook animals:** Give animals extra room and time to adjust to you. In passing, use special care and follow directions of horseback riders (ask if uncertain).
- Plan ahead: Know your equipment, your ability, and the area in which you are riding—and prepare accordingly.

HORSE PACKING: THE ULTIMATE CHALLENGE

Use of pack stock in the backcountry varies significantly with geographic region—in many places in the West, it is dominated by organized outfitters leading hunting trips; in some locations, it is individuals who live nearby in a rural area; and in other places, vacationing families rent the horses from concessionaires. But no matter where the domestic animals come from, there is no denying that widespread use of pack stock in the backcountry can result in very noticeable environmental impacts to the landscape and negatively influence the experience of other visitors.

Of all nonmotorized modes of travel in the backcountry, horse packing has the greatest potential for environmental damage. Numerous studies have documented the substantial erosion to trails and

This campsite, with an outhouse and hitching post, has been heavily impacted by horses. (photo by David Cole)

destruction to campsites caused by pack stock. On the other hand, Virgil Mink, a recreation wilderness manager with the Tonapah National Forest in Nevada and a self-proclaimed "guru" of Leave No Trace horse packing, maintains that he can take pack stock into the backcountry and create no more impact than a party of hikers.

"Traveling with horses can have a high impact on the land, but the challenges in reducing that impact are not insurmountable," said Mink in a recent conversation. Compared to backpacking, implementing Leave No Trace practices when horse packing poses some unique and difficult challenges. First, there is the sheer weight of the animal; 1,500 pounds bearing down on four hooves has the potential to inflict significant trampling damage on soil and vegetation. Second, horses poop a lot and they do not bury it in cat holes. Aside from this waste being an aesthetic problem for other backcountry users who do not like to step in it, horse manure often contains seeds that introduce ecologically damaging weed species to the environment. And then there is the fact that pack stock like to graze, which defoliates vegetation, and the animals have to be confined at camp, which can cause a mess.

For all these reasons, there has been a growing trend among land managers to limit or ban horses in wilderness areas. According to a 1993 U.S. Forest Service study of pack stock use, 6 of 308 wilderness areas (2 percent) in 1980 prohibited horse packing; by 1990 stock use was prohibited in 58 of 423 wilderness areas (14 percent). Although the number of designated wilderness areas across the United States increased, the number of these federal preserves that are open to horse packing declined.

Mink took on the cause of promoting and developing minimum-impact horsepacking techniques some five years ago when he was a Forest Service volunteer. "I am a longtime horse packer," he said, "and I could see the impact that pack stock were having on the environment, and that land managers were going to ban horses from more and more wilderness areas if things did not change."

Mink was not the only one concerned. The Backcountry Horsemen of America, a national equestrian organization with a broad membership (see the appendix), jumped on the minimum-impact bandwagon and began promoting to its members the environmentally sensitive approach to horse packing. The Leave No Trace staff at NOLS developed an LNT "Master" course designed specifically to teach minimum-impact horse packing techniques. They also produced an LNT "Backcountry Horse Use" booklet that is distributed to the public by land managers.

Today, the notion of minimizing impact when horse packing is no longer a novel concept and, in fact, there are riding clubs around the country that pride themselves on their environmental ethics and LNT practices. "I know in my district it has made a difference," said Mink. "People who have been gone two years and recently came back to this area say the forest looks better—they do not see the horse impacts like they used to."

Tying horses to trees and bushes damages vegetation. (photo by David Cole)

All of the six basic principles of the Leave No Trace program apply to horse packing, but there are also a host of specific practices that are vital to meeting the impact challenges inherent with pack stock. According to Mink, "The main thing is planning." This means finding out ahead of time from the land manager what horse restrictions are in place in the area you will be visiting, and packing as lightly and as smartly as possible. Following is a rundown of some of the key principles of LNT horse packing.

Learning to Pack Lightly

Traveling light reduces the number of pack animals you need to bring into the backcountry, which is key to minimizing impact.

- Rather than heavy canvas tents, bring lightweight nylon shelters.
- Opt for sleeping bags instead of cots.
- Try using a compact gas-fueled camp stove instead of cooking over a fire with a big Dutch oven.
- Pack freeze-dried and dehydrated meals in reusable plastic bags rather than throwing a bunch of canned goods and glass containers in your saddlebags. Mink even goes so far as to encourage people to put their libations in a lightweight flask instead of hauling the whole bottle.

Using Weed-free Feed

It is estimated that invasive weeds are spreading at a rate of 4,600 acres per day on federal lands—a problem that is largely due to seeds transmitted by pack animals.

- To help stem the spread of noxious weeds in wildlands and to reduce grazing damage to vegetation, bring supplemental feed for your animals that is "certified weed-free."
- Begin feeding your stock the certified weed-free grub two days before entering the backcountry to prevent the possibility of any noxious seeds from being transported through the animals' manure. (Using certified weed-free feed is required by land managers in some wilderness areas.)
- When in camp, it is also a good idea to feed your stock using a nose bag or manti. This helps the horse eat every last bite of its weed-free dinner and prevents the animal from roughing up the dirt to munch its meal off the ground.

Minimizing Trampling

Because of the inevitable trampling impact that results from horse travel, it is especially important for parties of pack stock users to stick to designated trails. Other methods for reducing trampling include:

- Avoid riding on trails during times of the year when you know much of the path will be muddy. And if you come upon a muddy patch, try to get your horse to go through the middle of it rather than around the muck, which further widens and erodes the trail.
- If you know you will be traveling on fairly even terrain, consider

This trail has been heavily trampled by horses. (photo by David Cole)

outfitting your horse with flat plate-style shoes before leaving home. Shoes with heel and toe caulks give horses better traction on steep, rocky, or icy slopes, but they also increase the potential for trail erosion.

- If you find it necessary to travel cross-country with your stock, make sure it is on a durable surface, like dry grassland, and allow your animals to travel abreast to spread trampling impacts rather than keeping them single file.

Resting Carefully

The challenge to minimize impacts during a horse packing trip never stops, even when you and your horses stop for a break. A variety of negative environmental and social impacts can occur in the span of just five minutes.

- When taking breaks, move your animals off the trail so others can get by.
- Hobble your horses rather than tying them to trees even if it is for just five minutes; a

horse tied to a tree trunk can break branches and permanently damage bark and roots.

- When watering your horses, keep the animals away from wet, marshy springs, streambanks, and the soggy edges of ponds and lakes. These areas are especially susceptible to trampling, erosion, and pollution. Try to let your animals drink from an established ford or find a low, rocky spot that is less susceptible to trampling. It is also helpful to bring a bucket for watering horses; just fill it up anywhere and let your stock drink 200 feet away from the water source, where trampling is not a concern.
- Before leaving the resting spot, scatter any horse droppings with a shovel or a swift kick of your boot.

The LNT Horse Camp

Choosing a campsite and a method for restraining horses in camp are easily the most important minimum-impact decisions a horse packer will make. Because confined animals can significantly scar an otherwise undisturbed backcountry location, it is best to set up camp at an established site—preferably one that is officially or unofficially designated for pack stock use, what Mink calls a "sacrifice site." Consult with the local land manager before your trip to find out where the best pack stock campsites are located.

When it comes to confining your stock, never tie them to trees. As a result of the damage horses cause to root systems and bark, this longtime practice has killed trees in backcountry areas heavily used by pack stock. Tying horses in this manner also damages the soil around the tree, creating a telltale "doughnut" pounded into the earth by the restless animal. The two best ways confine stock and minimize environmental impacts are:

The highline: This is the most popular Leave No Trace method for confining horses. It involves placing the horses in between two trees where there is little chance for trampling damage. To erect a highline, find an area around camp with dry, hardened ground and stretch a rope at a height a little over the horses' heads between two live trees that are at least 8 inches in diameter. To prevent the rope from girdling the trees, use adjustable nylon "tree saver" straps; gunny

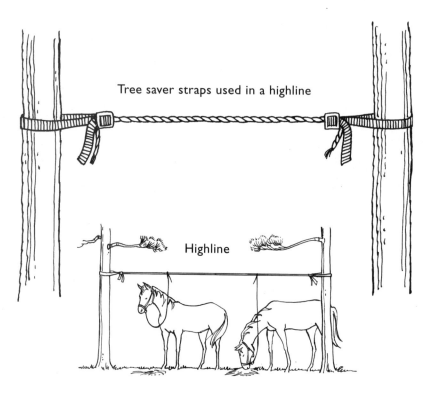

Tree saver straps used in a highline

Highline

sacks come in handy for additional bark padding if needed. Tie the animals' lead ropes at intervals along the highline, so that they are away from tree trunks and unable to slide along the line. Make sure the lead rope is long enough to allow the horse some movement, but not so much that it could wrap around the animal's neck or leg.

Electric fencing: Another restraining method—the personal preference of Mink—is to use portable electric fencing to create a temporary corral. The fencing is lightweight, powered by flashlight-size batteries, and very effective for pack stock that have already been trained to respect it.

Electric fence

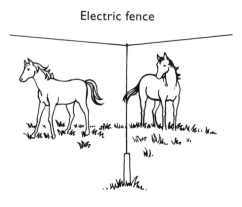

The traditional horse outfitter camp often uses big canvas wall tents. (photo by David Cole)

Regardless of which method you choose for confining your animals, keep them in that location for only one night to reduce trampling and grazing impacts, and be sure to scatter their turd piles when breaking camp.

As for the humans in camp, follow the minimum-impact procedures detailed in chapters 1, All About Camping, and 2, LNT Principles of Hygiene and the Wilderness Bathroom. This includes restricting the use of campfires, properly disposing of human waste, and packing out all garbage. One of the advantages of horse packing is it allows people to carry in various items that aid in efforts to minimize impact, such as fire pans, bear-proof food boxes, and portable latrines. And remember to respect the desires of others within hearing range who have likely come to the wilderness in search of peace and quiet.

Mink conceded that even though Leave No Trace practices are catching on with individual horse packers, many outfitters using pack stock are sticking to the old ways. "They have people who pay money with the expectation that they are going to camp like they have seen on the cowboy shows on TV," he said. "Those people want the big, walled canvas tents, the cots, and lots of Dutch oven cooking." Like most wilderness area land managers in the West, Mink attempts to confine the impacts of these outfitter groups by requiring them to camp at certain designated group sites.

However, the horse packing "guru" has also recently come up with another innovative way to keep stock users happy while significantly minimizing their impacts. "I have a special trailhead I like to show off," he said. "It has corrals, and I encourage people to camp there and go into the wilderness for day rides. Groups really like it; it has become a preferred spot for horse packers because they have everything they need there."

LNT Basics: Horse Packing

Pack Light

- Use modern camping equipment, including lightweight tents, sleeping bags, and stoves.
- Pack freeze-dried and dehydrated meals in reusable plastic bags rather than food in heavy cans and glass containers.

Use Weed-free Feed

- Feed your pack stock certified "weed-free" feed—both in camp and before leaving on your trip.

Minimize Trampling

- Avoid riding on trails during times of year when you know much of the path will be muddy.
- If you come upon a muddy patch, try to get your horse to go through the middle of it rather than around the muck.
- When traveling on fairly even terrain, consider outfitting your horse with flat plate-style shoes before leaving home.

- During rest breaks, hobble your horses rather than tying them to trees.
- When watering your horses, keep the animals away from wet, marshy springs, streambanks, and the soggy edges of ponds and lakes. Try to let your animals drink from an established ford or find a low, rocky spot that is less susceptible to trampling.

The Horse Camp

- Minimize impacts when camping by choosing the most durable site. Camp at a site designated for pack stock whenever possible.
- Confine your horses in electric fencing or with a highline.
- Scatter horse droppings when vacating the site.
- Stay at a site for only one night, and then move on.

CHAPTER 5

MINIMIZING IMPACTS ON WATERWAYS

LNT Guidelines for Sea Kayakers, Canoeists, and Rafters

BECAUSE MOST OF OUR PLANET IS WATER, it would seem as though there is more than enough room for all boaters to roam without bumping into each other or negatively impacting the environment. But most paddlers travel on a very small percentage of the earth's wet stuff, typically hugging popular wilderness coastlines and floating the precious few undammed stretches of scenic rivers. Consequently, the concentration of users in places like coastal barrier islands, canyon river corridors, and lakeshore campsites offers quite a challenge when it comes to Leave No Trace practices.

To further complicate matters, backcountry paddling—whether it is kayaking, canoeing, or rafting—lends itself to traveling in groups and taking lots of stuff. This need not be inherently damaging to the environment, especially if some of that stuff includes LNT tools like a fire pan and a portable potty, but such waterborne group pursuits require special minimum-impact considerations on the part of the user.

On the plus side, nonmotorized water travel does not have the same kind of user conflicts that are currently raging among ground-based wilderness users. In most places, kayakers, canoeists, and even

A kayaker pulls into a backcountry campsite on the Colorado River, AZ/CA. (photo by Chris Gould)

large parties of rafters all seem to get along swimmingly. The key is for all these different types of paddlers to travel and camp the LNT way so that heavily visited boating destinations will continue to be enjoyable. After all, nothing will sink a great float trip faster than lots of litter along a riverbank or human waste washing up onshore.

▲ ▲ ▲

How We Play

According to the 1995 "State of the Industry Report" published by the trade group Outdoor Recreation Coalition of America (ORCA), more than 75 percent of all Americans age sixteen and older participate in some form of outdoor recreation. This includes people walking around their neighborhood and biking in city parks, but it also encompasses a multitude of specialized outdoor pursuits that are becoming increasingly popular and are possible, in large part, through access to public lands.

The longtime favorites of tent camping and day hiking remain the most popular activities on our giant, albeit sometimes crowded, 700-million-acre playground of federal public lands. According to figures of the National Sporting Goods Association (NSGA), camping claimed some 43 million participants in 1995, and day hikers across the nation numbered 25 million. Other popular backcountry sports (according to 1995 NSGA figures) are backpacking, with 10.2 million participants; canoeing, with 7.2 million participants; off-road mountain biking, with 5.7 million participants; climbing, with 4 million participants; cross-country skiing, with 3.4 million participants, and kayaking or rafting, with 2.5 million participants.

While the more traditional outdoor activities like hiking, camping, and horseback riding continue to experience slight annual increases in popularity, newer mainstream sports— namely mountain biking, rock climbing, and white-water paddling—are growing by leaps and bounds. Also making a surprise comeback, according to the ORCA report, is cross-country skiing, which experienced a downturn in the 1980s, but is now one of the fastest-growing outdoor activities in the United States.

SEA KAYAKING: PADDLING SOFTLY IN COASTAL ENVIRONMENTS

Sea kayaking has grown rapidly in popularity over the last decade and is having a significant impact on fragile island environments on both the Atlantic and Pacific Coasts, from Maine to Baja. "We are overwhelmed with recreational use," said Sid Quarrier, a volunteer for the Maine Island Trail Association (MITA). "Even though most kayakers try to act in an environmentally responsible manner, the islands are just being taxed through sheer visitor numbers."

The Maine Island Trail is a water route that strings together some 80 designated islands (out of 3,000) along 350 miles of coastline. Although about half of the islands are open to the general public because they are state-owned, the balance are privately owned and open only to MITA members. Most of the islands on the trail are small—about an acre—and uninhabited. The isolated environments and wildlife populations on these islands are particularly fragile, and MITA devotes much of its staff and volunteer time to educating trail users on how to minimize their impacts. MITA enlists volunteers who monitor specific islands and frequently visit campsites to talk to paddlers about LNT practices. MITA also publishes a guidebook, half of which is devoted to explaining how to minimize environmental impacts when visiting the islands. (To contact MITA, see the appendix.)

Making Camp

Coastal environments can vary greatly depending on where you are on the planet. The forested shores of Alaska, for example, are a far cry from the desert beaches of Baja. Nevertheless, all coastlines have one thing in common: an intertidal zone—a zone that is the most resistant of all natural surfaces to human impacts.

In some situations, you may not be able to access this tidal area due to steep cliffs or wildlife activity. But whenever possible, conduct all your activities in the intertidal zone; this includes camping, fire building, hiking, and sanitation. Beyond this one maxim, follow these guidelines to minimize your impact when on a sea kayaking trip:

- When coming and going between land and water, launch and land your vessel on sandy beaches or sloping rock ledges. Scrambling over dirt banks and shrubby ledges promotes erosion that continues long after you have pushed off.

- On the shoreline, choose an established campsite in the intertidal zone if such an option is available.
- Make sure your campsite is above the daily high tide line so you do not get washed away, but, preferably below the monthly high tide mark (tides are highest during the period of a new moon and full moon).
- When hiking outside the intertidal zone, stick to durable surfaces such as rocks or an established trail.
- Due to the fragile soils and lack of wood, combined with high visitor use, campfires are generally bad news on islands and should be avoided. Do your cooking and hand warming on a camp stove. It may be appropriate to build a fire on a coastal beach, below high tide, if there is plenty of driftwood available, and if fires are permitted.

Kayaking on the Colorado River (photo by Chris Gould)

Waste Disposal

In coastal environments that are not heavily used by humans, the oceans can act as a natural wastewater treatment system, making "going to the bathroom" quite simple. As for urination, just do it anywhere below the high tide line and away from tidal pools and other people.

Solid waste management requires a little more discretion. It is illegal to discharge human waste into U.S. waters. If conditions permit, bury your waste, cat-hole style (see chapter 2, LNT Principles of Hygiene and the Wilderness Bathroom), just above the high tide line where the temperate coastal soils will speed decomposition.

Dealing with solid waste on islands that receive frequent visitors, however, is a different story—and an environmental challenge that MITA is all too familiar with. The LNT guidelines set out by the association could apply to most coastal island environments in North America: All poop should be packed out. The soils on the islands are shallow and fragile; "one footprint on a lichen bed could last ten years," said Quarrier. Plus, in the space of just one acre, there is not much room for cat holes when people are camping on the islands every night during prime seasons. If you are camping on an island anywhere in the Lower 48, chances are you should pack out your poop. Here are some of the preferred packing methods used by veteran paddlers.

The poop tube: A common item among big wall climbers, the poop tube works just as well for packing out waste on kayak trips. This is a homemade contraption comprised of PVC pipe parts that can be purchased at most hardware stores.

- The PVC pipe should be about 4 inches in diameter and cut to size, anywhere from 12 to 25 inches in length (depending on your personal habits and how long you are going to be out there). Have one end threaded, or get a threaded fitting.
- Glue a cap on one end, using the recommended PVC cement, and glue a threaded fitting on the other end if the pipe itself is not threaded. Get a plug for the other end that screws into the pipe threads.
- Using duct tape and some nylon cord, fashion a loop through the top of the plug and attach it to the pipe. This will prevent the plug from getting lost and it will give you a means for tying the tube to a secure spot.

- Do your pooping in brown paper bags, toss in a little kitty litter for odor control, and stuff it in the tube for safe keeping. At the end of your trip, dispose of the contents of the tube in a vault toilet or at an RV dump station.

A one-gallon plastic, resealable container: Use it with a little seawater in it.

A waterproof ammo canister: Line it with a garbage bag.

A biodegradable bag: Carry kitty litter, sand, or leaves in another container.

A bucket with a tight-fitting lid: Use for groups.

An ample-sized resealable plastic container: One veteran MITA member prefers to deposit her waste on a turfy spot where there are plenty of leaves, sand, or loose soil. She rolls the poop in the substrate and scoops it up with toilet paper or a baggie over the hand, then transfers the stuff to the container. She rinses out the hand baggie in salt water for reuse. She finds her system an innocuous approach to packing it out because the poop is well hidden by the leaves and dirt.

But there are also many other ways to pack it out, and it seems sea kayakers, more than any other recreational group, have a knack for coming up with innovative techniques for transporting their poop. Just keep in mind that it is illegal to dispose of human waste in a dumpster or any trash facility that is not ultimately headed for a sewage treatment plant.

Protecting Wildlife

A major environmental concern for sea kayakers is wildlife impacts. Although paddling may seem less intrusive than boats with noisy outboard motors, just the mere presence of humans is often perceived as a threat by coastal wildlife. Kayakers on the Maine Island Trail, for example, share the territory with populations of seals, sea lions, eagles, and various seabirds, including murres, puffins, and cormorants.

Many islands with nesting populations of these species are closed to camping during especially sensitive periods. Paddlers are asked to avoid seabird nesting sites from early April to mid-August, and to steer clear of seal populations from mid-May through mid-June, when the animals bear their young. Intrusion into nesting or breeding areas during these times can be devastating to wildlife.

Litter left by rafting revelers on the Salt River, AZ (photo by Mike Frick)

For instance, seals and sea lions haul out on land to form colonies where they give birth and nurse their young. Just one kayak venturing too close to a haul-out site can start a panicked stampede, causing most of the pups to be crushed to death as the adults rush to the water for safety. And even if there are only a few adult seals on shore, the approach of one kayak could cause a mother and her pup to run for the water. In the state of panic, there is a good chance the pup could be separated from its mother, which would lead to its eventual death.

Respect all posted wildlife restrictions when paddling in coastal areas, and be especially cautious during the spring and summer months. If you see a seal raise its head to look at you, then you are too close. A general rule for most marine wildlife species is to maintain a buffer of at least 100 yards no matter what time of year you are on the water. Invest in good binoculars and a telephoto lens for your camera; this will allow you to view and photograph wildlife species without inadvertently harassing them.

LNT Basics: Sea Kayaking

Making Camp

- Try to conduct all camping, hiking, and hygiene activities in the intertidal zone.
- When coming and going between land and water, land and launch your vessel on sandy beaches or sloping rock ledges.
- Do not build fires on islands. Avoid building a fire on coastal beaches unless there is an abundance of driftwood, and fires are permitted.

Waste Disposal

- In remote coastal environments, dispose of human waste by burying it in a cat hole above the high tide line.
- When camping on popular barrier islands, pack out your poop in a poop tube or other container.
- Urinate anywhere that is below the high tide line and away from other people.

Protect Wildlife

- Be aware of wildlife impacts. Avoid seabird nesting sites from early April to mid-August, and steer clear of seal populations from mid-May through mid-June, when the animals bear their young.
- A general rule for most marine wildlife species is to maintain a buffer of at least 100 yards no matter what time of year you are on the water.

CANOEING AND RAFTING: ROWING YOUR BOAT GENTLY

Rafting and canoeing on backcountry rivers are also increasingly popular modes of wilderness travel. Of course, people have been using America's waterways to get around for thousands of years, and before the advent of pavement, river corridors were our nation's primary transportation routes.

Because of their utilitarian role, most rivers in the United States have been developed and no longer resemble the pristine riparian environments of several centuries ago. In fact, of the 3 million miles of rivers and streams in the United States, only 0.3 percent are protected as wilderness waterways under the National Wild and Scenic Rivers System. And it is this tiny fraction of wilderness rivers that most paddlers want to visit.

Always abide by regulations when whale-watching.
(photo © Dorcas Miller)

The fact that river travelers are all floating down the same corridors offers some advantages and disadvantages from an LNT perspective. The use is inevitably concentrated, so—unlike popular backpacking destinations where hikers roam everywhere—environmental destruction on rivers is generally contained. But large groups of people all boating in the same area creates social and environmental challenges, especially when it comes to managing human waste, controlling litter, and minimizing camping impacts.

These days, canoeing and rafting on popular rivers often comes with plenty of land management regulations. It may seem like a hassle to follow all the different minimum-impact procedures, but one need only look at the tidy condition of the Colorado River through the Grand Canyon to see that it is worth it.

Making Camp

It is a common management policy on popular rivers to require visitors to camp at designated sites. The objective, of course, is to concentrate use—which is a good idea regardless of whether the land manager requires you to do it.

If you happen to be traveling on a more remote river and cannot find a well-established site, set up camp within the floodplain on beaches or gravel bars. However, if you are traveling during a period of heavy rain or snowmelt and know the water level could rise suddenly and significantly, choose a campsite on a durable surface well above the river.

Maybe it is because canoes and, especially, rafts have the capacity for carrying lots of stuff that the potential for people on river trips to accidentally litter is high. Try to repackage foods before the trip so you reduce your littering potential. Once in camp, consider laying a tarp down as a "kitchen floor" to catch debris that might otherwise get buried in the sand.

Vegetation in riparian environments is especially sensitive, and seedlings usually do not stand a chance in and around popular riverside campsites. When in camp, try to conduct as much of your activity as possible below the river's floodplain or in heavily impacted areas.

Campfires are a problem in river environments primarily because of the lack of wood at established campsites. If you want to have a fire, bring in your own wood or pick up driftwood over the course of the day's paddle. Use a fire pan, and locate the fire on a beach or gravel bar (see chapter 1, All About Camping, for more on fire-building practices). Many land managers require use of a fire pan and ask that all ashes and charcoal be packed out.

Rafting on the Salt River, AZ (photo by Chris Gould)

Waste Disposal

If you happen to be on a remote river where you can dig a cat hole at least 200 feet from shore, go ahead and bury your waste. But because of the popularity of many waterways—and the fact that numerous Western rivers go through narrow, slickrock canyons—it has become standard procedure (and, in the West, land management policy) for most boaters to pack out their waste. Fortunately, rafts and canoes have a large carrying capacity and are ideally suited for hauling portable toilets to pack out the group poop.

Sanitary conditions on the Colorado River in the Grand Canyon got pretty bad before rafting outfitters came around to wholeheartedly supporting the "pack it out" principle. A 1972 poll of Grand Canyon river runners, "Use and Quality of Wildland Water," showed that more than half of those surveyed said they had contracted some form of gastrointestinal illness when on the job. As beautiful as the setting of the canyon might appear, there were obviously just too many people leaving behind too much poop.

"We were always digging up other people's dump sites, and toilet paper was everywhere," recalled longtime river rat and Grand Canyon National Park wilderness supervisor Kim Crumbo in a recent conversation; Crumbo worked as a guide in the canyon in the early '70s. Most folks in the rafting community agreed there was only one option—aside from severely restricting the number of people on the river—and that was to pack out human waste.

In 1979, when Crumbo joined the Grand Canyon National Park staff, it had become Park Service policy and standard outfitter procedure to pack out all poop on river trips. Old ammo "rocket" boxes were used as the receptacles; often they were equipped with a removable toilet seat for customer comfort. And the honor of slop duty usually went to the most junior guide on the trip. Today, the number of people rafting through the canyon has grown to 23,000 annually, but the river environment is far cleaner than it was back in the early '70s—and the guides are not getting sick.

Since the poop packing rule was first implemented in the Grand Canyon in the late 1970s, a host of companies have developed a variety of portable potties designed primarily for river travel. A good, up-to-

This LNT bathroom at a kayaker's basecamp still offers some of the comforts of home without harming the environment.
(photo © Dorcas Miller)

date summary of what is available in this growing market can be found in *How to Shit in the Woods*, by Kathleen Meyer. Here are some of the highlights from Meyer's plethora of potty options now available to the paddling public:

A molded-plastic holding tank: This comes with aluminum handles, a hard plastic seat assembly, and easy-to-clean parts.

A stainless-steel holding tank: This comes with an automatic pressure release valve and an opening for freshwater flushing. Some models have stout handles at seat level; combined with a square design, this provides stability for those on the throne.

A chemical resistant, laminated fiberglass resin seat tank: This comes with marine-grade fasteners and handles, and a hose fitting that serves as the venting system when in camp.

A stainless-steel box with a standard toilet seat: This fits neatly into any old 20-millimeter "rocket" box. It has a built-in power spray nozzle that blasts the inside when emptying at a dump station, while the quick-release top lid remains sealed, virtually assuring the handler of no unpleasant doodoo contact.

A lightweight, high-density polyethylene bucket: This has a screw-type transport lid with a safety lock, and no pressure release valve.

A biodegradable pot and lid: Made out of recycled paper, this unique contraption comes with five additional form-fitting disks that are pressed into place over each day's deposits. To use the device, place the disks inside a five-gallon pickle pail and put the toilet seat on top.

No matter which type you decide on, keep in mind that before you head down the river with the latrine in tow, you should find out from the land manager where you can properly empty your potty at the end of your trip.

Because of the high number of people traveling and camping along a river corridor, the stench of urine can sometimes be a problem on popular waterways. The solution in some cases, such as in the Grand Canyon, is a land management policy that instructs visitors to pee directly in the water. This is an environmentally sound practice in any large, silty, high-volume Western river.

On other rivers that are located in parts of the country where rainfall is more likely to dilute the urine smell, just walk a good distance away from camp to do your peeing.

Reducing Impact

Be sure to lash down everything in your boat. In the unexpected event of capsizing, you will be able to keep your gear and prevent sending expensive litter downriver.

If you decide to go for an exploratory hike from camp, stick to established trails—which are certain to exist at well-used sites.

LNT Basics: Canoeing and Rafting

Making Camp

- Try to camp in the river's floodplain (unless there is risk of flooding), and check with land managers about designated sites.
- Control litter by repackaging foods before the trip and putting down a tarp in the camp cooking area to catch debris.
- Avoid having a campfire. If you do, use a fire pan; bring wood with you or pick up driftwood for fuel over the course of the day.

Waste Disposal

- On remote, rarely visited waterways, bury your waste in a cat hole 200 feet from shore.
- If you are traveling through a narrow, slickrock river corridor or in a popular area, pack out your solid waste.
- On silty Western rivers, urinate in the waterway; otherwise, pee well away from shore and campsites.

Reducing Impact

- Secure your load in the boat to avoid littering in the event of a capsize.
- Be aware of trampling impacts to vegetation, and follow established trails when venturing away from the river corridor.

CHAPTER 6

SPECIAL ENVIRONMENTS

Artic Tundra, Alpine Tundra, Deserts, and Archaeological Sites

WHEN AUTHOR AND ECO-WARRIOR Edward Abbey wrote *Desert Solitaire* in the mid-1960s, it was something of a novelty to celebrate hiking in the harsh environs of the desert. Back then, the deserts and other wilderness areas considered a "no-man's land" were backcountry destinations only for the eccentric. While Abbey was wandering alone among the cacti, most hikers stuck to the picture postcard places—the alpine meadows, lush forests, and backcountry lakes.

Abbey was ahead of his time. As more and more people ventured into the wilderness, the further afield folks traveled to find solitude and a sense of adventure. Places generally considered inhospitable to humans became sought-after destinations, from the frozen Arctic to windblown mountaintops to the arid desert. Now these extreme environments are on the must-visit list for many wilderness travelers, and people are crowding spots that Ed Abbey used to explore all by his lonesome.

Arctic tundra, alpine tundra (above tree line), and deserts have several things in common: the harsh terrain is generally not conducive to supporting human life, and—compared to all other types of landscapes—the terrain is least able to withstand impacts from human visitors. When hikers travel across tundra or sensitive desert soils, trampling impacts can last several hundred years, rather than years or decades in a forest or meadow environment.

This does not mean that human visitors should necessarily stay away from these extremely sensitive environments. On the contrary, there is no place I would rather be backpacking than in the scenic desert wilderness areas of Arizona and southern Utah. But visiting these places requires an understanding of the fragile environment in which you are traveling and knowledge of LNT skills aimed specifically at minimizing impact there.

What follows are some guidelines for hiking and camping in tundra and desert landscapes, as well as some pointers for minimizing impact around archaeological sites. Primarily found in Southwestern deserts, these ancient ruins are irreplaceable and highly susceptible to decay. Consequently, the presence of these cultural treasures makes an already fragile environment that much more vulnerable to human impacts.

▲ ▲ ▲

U.S. Fish and Wildlife Service and Bureau of Land Management
Two Agencies with Multiple-use Missions but Plenty of Wilderness

When most people plan a backcountry trip, they may only consider visiting Forest Service or national park lands. What they may not know, however, is that the U.S. Fish and Wildlife Service and the Bureau of Land Management have plenty of backcountry areas that are excellent recreation destinations—and they typically have far fewer visitors.

Preserves managed by the U.S. Fish and Wildlife Service may not be as heavily inundated by human visitors, but the refuges see plenty of traffic from feathered species. Established by Congress in 1956 to run the nation's wildlife refuge system, the Fish and Wildlife Service currently oversees the management of 90 million acres in seventy-five preserves.

However, 85 percent (77 million acres) of the refuge system
is in Alaska. The remaining refuges in the Lower 48 states
are primarily located along the four major North American
flyways—Atlantic, Central, Mississippi, and Pacific—and are
critical rest stops for migrating birds.

Although these national wildlife refuges have been established to protect shrinking habitat for certain species, "secondary uses" allowed on many of the preserves—such as
hunting, off-road vehicle usage, and water skiing—are harmful to wildlife. For example, military bombing exercises regularly conducted on the Cabeza Prieta National Wildlife
Refuge in Arizona are the source of major stress for antelope
and other wildlife; proposed oil drilling on the Arctic National
Wildlife Refuge in Alaska would threaten, among other species, migrating caribou herds.

The Bureau of Land Management (BLM) oversees 272
million acres, which is a larger portion of federal lands
(about 45 percent) than any other agency. Located almost
entirely in the Western Lower 48 states and Alaska, the vast
BLM holdings comprise what is left of the public domain and
can generally be characterized as the "leftover lands"—the
land that was too inhospitable to be homesteaded and is
lacking in lush, loggable forests and any notable "crown
jewel"–type features that would make it worthy of a national
park. However, for lovers of solitude and wild places, BLM
lands offer a wealth of recreation destinations.

Established in 1946 when Congress merged the U.S. Grazing Service and General Land Office, the BLM has historically
been involved in the business of managing federal real estate
for the benefit of private ranchers and mining companies. It
was not until the passage of the Federal Land Policy and
Management Act in 1976 that the BLM was formally dis-
charged of the 150-year-old duty of "disposing" of the public
domain. The landmark law gave the BLM statutory authority
to retain and manage all that was left of the public domain in

the best interest of its owners—the public. The law also instructed the BLM to inventory its holdings for lands that should be added to the National Wilderness Preservation System, a charge the agency had been excluded from when the Wilderness Act was passed in 1964.

Over the past two decades, recreation has become a growing component of the BLM's multiple-use mandate. These undeveloped lands, especially in the Southwest, are increasingly popular destinations for backpacking, mountain biking, and camping, among other activities. Currently, BLM holdings encompass some 470 developed recreation sites and more than 2,000 miles of trails. The agency is the steward of the new 1.7-million-acre Grand Staircase–Escalante National Monument located in southern Utah, established in 1996 by President Clinton.

ARCTIC TUNDRA

Treeless, level, or rolling ground in polar regions is known as arctic tundra. This type of terrain occupies 10 percent of the earth's surface area, with a large part of that amount found in Alaskan and Canadian wilderness. Arctic tundra is a polar desert, of sorts; the sparse vegetation has a growing season only two to four months long, and precipitation is usually less than 15 inches per year.

Existing at high latitudes, an arctic tundra ecosystem is subjected to long periods of sunlight in summer and darkness in winter, and extreme temperature fluctuations—sometimes going from 40 degrees Fahrenheit in summer to -25 degrees in winter. Plant life that can live in this harsh climate includes hearty species such as lichens, mosses, small herbs, and low shrubs. Animals common to arctic tundra are the polar bear, arctic fox, arctic wolf, arctic weasel, and caribou. And, as anyone who has visited the Arctic National Wildlife Refuge in summer knows, mosquitoes and blackflies seem more plentiful in an arctic tundra environment than anywhere else on the planet.

Although the arctic tundra landscape generally stays frozen year-round, the top layer of soil thaws in the summer months, causing water

Arctic tundra is characterized by a treeless landscape.
(photo © Dorcas Miller)

to permeate down to an ice and soil barrier called permafrost. Because the water has nowhere to go, it stays pooled just above the permafrost barrier, causing the top thawed layer of soil to be quite mushy. It is during this thaw period that most of the biological activity that sustains the tundra ecosystem takes place: animals burrow into the soil, plant roots extend down, and organic matter decomposes into food or microorganisms. The web of life in an arctic tundra environment is very delicate, and any of these processes can be easily upset by human visitors, thereby causing a domino effect that will degrade the ecosystem.

Traveling on Arctic Tundra
Aside from the fact that slogging through wet tundra makes for very difficult hiking, the potential for eroding this fragile landscape is extreme. Areas blanketed with sensitive vegetation such as lichen beds or woody, stemmed groundcovers are the most at risk. Researchers studying visitor impacts in Alaska's central Brooks Range ("The Arrigetch Peaks Region of the Central Brooks Range, Alaska") found, for example, that once hikers trampled a lichen colony, soil beds that took hundreds of years to develop were lost to erosion.

The unique way in which arctic tundra erodes from trampling is called thermokarsting. When protective groundcover plants are destroyed, it exposes the soil to more sunlight and causes too many ice crystals in the permafrost layer to melt. Because ice has a higher volume than water, the unnatural thawing causes the top soil layer to sink, and makes it nearly impossible for vegetation to ever re-establish itself. Once thermokarsting occurs, it is likely a permanent change to the landscape.

In her book *Midnight Wilderness*, Debbie Miller talks about encountering thermokarsting in the early 1990s while walking across the tundra in Alaska's Arctic National Wildlife Refuge. The scars from a truck that drove through the area in the 1950s were clearly visible and its tracks had eroded into the soil about 6 inches.

Practicing the LNT principle of "camp and travel on durable surfaces" is critical when visiting an arctic tundra environment—but a durable surface is not always easy to find. Unfortunately, the summer months that are most hospitable to humans is also the time when the land is at its mushiest state and most susceptible to trampling.

Whenever possible, hike on established trails. In the absence of established pathways, seek out boulder-strewn streambeds as the next best durable surface for your route. If, after considering all the options, you find it necessary to travel across the tundra, try to walk on ground that is dry and covered with grasses or sedges rather than low shrubs or lichen beds. As in other places, when traveling cross-country on arctic tundra, spread out rather than walking single file and try to stick to durable surfaces like snow or rock.

Making Camp

The terrain that is most suitable for hiking in an arctic tundra environment is also the best choice for camp. If you have the option of camping at an established site, do so. However, the chances of finding established campsites in most arctic wilderness areas are not very great, and the next best option is to camp in the gravel bed of a stream drainage—as long as you take precautions against flash floods and are at least 200 feet from the water.

If flooding is a possibility or there is no stream where you are traveling, seek out a patch of mineral soil to camp on for the night. On many tundra landscapes that are slightly hilly, soil slippage is a common occurrence, and exposed mineral soil makes for a durable and comfortable campsite.

Because of the lack of downed wood and the fragile soils on most arctic tundra landscapes, fires are inappropriate. Bring a camp stove for cooking and plenty of adequate clothing and gear for warmth.

Waste Disposal

Arctic wilderness is one of the few places on the planet where smearing feces may be the best poop placement option. Because tundra soils are so fragile and often frozen, digging a cat hole can be problematic in remote areas of Alaska and Canada, and other arctic regions as well.

Surface disposal should only be used if visitation to the region is very low and you are visiting the tundra environment during summer when there is plenty of sunlight to speed decomposition. Choose a spot for smearing that is 200 feet from marsh or bog areas so the water is not contaminated.

If you are visiting a popular area in the Arctic, dispose of waste in a cat hole when possible. Or, if the ground is frozen, packing it out may prove to be the most environmentally responsible option.

ALPINE TUNDRA

While arctic tundra is found at high *latitudes,* alpine tundra environments exist at high *altitudes*—in mountain ranges above tree line. You will encounter alpine tundra on many mountaintops in the Lower 48, including New Hampshire's White Mountains, the Adirondacks, the Rockies, the Sierras, and the Cascades. Like arctic tundra, this alpine landscape is treeless and most of the ecosystem-sustaining processes take place during a brief summer thaw period. The primary differences between alpine and arctic landscapes are that alpine soils are not perennially frozen and the precipitation is greater.

Because of harsh conditions, including wind gusts that can be hurricane force and a regular battering of lightning strikes, life above tree line is impossible for most species. There are, however, some hearty flora and fauna that manage to survive, and even thrive.

The most characteristic vegetation marking the boundaries of alpine tundra is called krummholz—twisted, dwarflike trees that are often thousands of years old. In addition to the diminutive and ancient trees, alpine tundra often harbors shrubs, lichens, and various types of wildflowers.

Alpine animals are only partially adapted to their harsh tundra environment and either migrate down-mountain or hibernate during winter. Species in alpine environs include mountain goats, bobcats, marmots, and voles.

Because of the struggle these plants and animals must endure just to survive, any kind of disturbance from human visitors can have severe consequences.

Traveling Above Tree Line

From the White Mountains to the Colorado Rockies to the Sierra Nevadas, it is the nature of alpine trails to be comprised of an endless chain of switchbacks to the summit. And it is human nature to try to take the quicker route by shortcutting up the switchbacks and pioneering

Wearing gaiters makes hiking on muddy or slushy alpine trails easier. (photo © Deborah Sussex, courtesy of NOLS)

"volunteer" trails. On popular summit trails, these renegade paths can literally destroy the delicate alpine tundra environment. Researchers in Rocky Mountain National Park, for example, have estimated that alpine tundra disturbed by informal trails could take several hundred to a thousand years to recover—even if the paths were never used again.

Hikers should stay on the trail no matter where they are, but it is imperative when traveling through alpine tundra. The fragile vegetation and micro-climates beneath rocks simply cannot withstand human disturbance. Wear gaiters—and crampons, if necessary—so you can walk through mud, snow, and ice on the trail rather than around it. Staying on the trail is a land management regulation in various popular alpine destinations, including the White Mountains in New Hampshire and Arizona's San Francisco Peaks.

Making Camp

In general, places above tree line do not make ideal campsites. There are the wind and exposure to lightning, and it is nearly impossible to spend the night on fragile alpine tundra without negatively impacting the environment.

If you find it necessary to pitch your tent above tree line, however, try to do it at an established site. It is common in popular mountain ranges to find campsites near the top with boulders moved around and a telltale fire ring. When an established site is not available, choose a resistant surface such as snow, rock, or mineral soil. Avoid disturbing vegetation and do not move rocks around—these are important micro-habitats in an alpine tundra environment.

Also, because of the typically strong gusts of wind on mountaintops, pay close attention to keeping track of your trash. A food bar wrapper or even a freestanding tent can quickly become airborne and sail off the mountain. As in the arctic tundra environment, campfires are a bad idea above tree line due to the obvious lack of fuel and the sensitive soils.

Waste Disposal

Surface disposal—or smearing—can in theory work in an alpine tundra setting for all the same reasons that it works in the arctic, but in reality it is not a good choice on mountaintops. There are too many people

When camping above treeline, choose a rocky rather than a vegetated surface. (photo © Deborah Sussex, courtesy of NOLS)

climbing around on popular peaks, and nobody wants to encounter someone else's smear. Consequently, land managers now require hikers and climbers on most popular mountains, like Mount Shasta and El Capitan in California, to pack out their poop. And even if it is not required, packing it out still may very likely be the best option in alpine tundra. An alternative may be hiking down to tree line or into a side canyon and finding suitable mineral or organic soil for digging a cat hole.

DESERTS

From the lush, botanical garden-type environment in Arizona's Organ Pipe Cactus National Monument to the endless plain of dry mudflats in California's Death Valley, desert terrain can vary dramatically in the United States. But the one thing the 500,000 square miles of desert in North America share is a scarcity of water. Just as the limited warmth makes tundra environments so fragile, it is the limited water in the desert that makes life extremely precarious for plants and animals in these arid lands. And as in tundra environments, the balance of life in desert ecosystems is far too delicate to withstand human impacts when the struggle to survive is already tough enough.

Deserts in North America generally fall into five different regions—all located west of the Mississippi. These various desert environments each have their own unique vegetation, climate, and terrain. When planning a desert backcountry trip, it is helpful to have an understanding of the environmental characteristics of the area in which you will be traveling so you can be prepared to practice LNT principles. Here is a summary of the desert regions you might visit:

Great Basin: The coldest, highest, largest, and northernmost of our continent's deserts, the Great Basin encompasses most of Nevada and Utah, and extends into southeastern Oregon, southern Idaho, southwestern Wyoming, the northwestern corner of Colorado, and a small portion of northern Arizona. Temperatures in the Great Basin are lower than in other deserts, and periods of freezing temperatures are not uncommon in winter. Great Basin vegetation is characterized by gray-green sagebrush and shadscale; these low-lying shrubs cover hundreds of square miles in continuous sweeps.

Mohave Desert: Situated primarily in southeastern California, the Mohave Desert is something of a transition zone between the Great Basin to the north and the Sonoran Desert to the south. Creosote bush is the most predominant vegetation in this sparse desert, but the distinctive Joshua tree is, perhaps, what gives the region the most notoriety. Joshua Tree National Park is a popular rock climbing destination in the Mohave.

Sonoran Desert: When Hollywood makes a Western, it is usually the Sonoran Desert that is the backdrop. The Sonoran Desert is rich

Sonoran desert vegetation—East Cactus Plain Wilderness Area, AZ
(photo by Mike Frick)

with a variety of vegetation, including the saguaro cactus, organ pipe cactus, palo verde, and many other spiny plants. The region spans southwestern Arizona, Baja California, and the northwestern coast of the Gulf of Mexico. Among the most beautiful destinations in the Sonoran Desert are Organ Pipe National Monument and the Superstition Mountain Wilderness Area in Arizona.

Chihuahuan Desert: Spanning southwestern Texas, southern New Mexico, and north-central Mexico, the Chihuahuan Desert is not as extremely dry as the other types of desert environments. Yucca and agave plants are common, as are mesquite and prickly pear cactus. Big Bend National Park in Texas offers excellent hiking opportunities in the Chihuahuan Desert.

Colorado Plateau: This arid region encompassing northern Arizona, southern Utah, northwestern New Mexico, and southwestern Colorado is actually a combination of Great Basin and Mohave Desert environments, but it has a character all its own. In fact, this high desert landscape, with its colorful sandstone arches, dramatic canyons, and scenic riparian corridors, probably receives more backcountry visitors than all other desert areas combined. Popular destinations in this region include Arizona's Grand Canyon National Park, Utah's Zion and Canyonlands National Parks, and numerous national monuments established to preserve ancient Native American cultural sites.

Desert Travel

For people who are unfamiliar with desert environments, the clumpy, black soil called cryptobiotic crust looks fairly insignificant. But, in fact, these irregularly raised pedestals in the sand are self-sustaining biological communities that are essential to the ecology of arid lands. Cryptobiotic crusts (also called cryptogam or cryptogamic soil) prevent erosion, enrich the soil, and allow new plants to take root. A mature cryptobiotic garden can take hundreds of years to develop, and human trampling can destroy it in just a few seconds. These delicate crusts are most prevalent on the Colorado Plateau, but are also common in the Sonoran Desert and Great Basin regions.

The number-one priority when traveling in the desert is to avoid stepping on cryptobiotic soil. It is not hard to do if you are looking out for this distinctive groundcover. The best option, from an LNT perspective, is to faithfully hike on established trails. If you find yourself in a region without trails, slickrock and gravel or sand washes are the most durable and suitable surfaces.

Also, try to minimize unnecessary hiking by being prepared. Check with land managers ahead of time about water availability in the region you are visiting, and pack in plenty of water. If you have enough water and/or you know where to find an adequate water source, you can avoid a lot of senseless and destructive roaming around looking for the elusive H_2O. Most desert travelers should plan on carrying at least one gallon of water per person per day on a desert trek.

Make sure you are familiar with the trail and route, so you do not

Established trail in high desert (southern Utah) through crytobiotic soil (photo by David Cole)

get lost and find yourself standing in the middle of a giant patch of cryptobiotic crust.

Making Camp

The same criteria used for desert travel also apply to finding a minimum-impact campsite. Whenever possible, camp at an established site. If that is not an option, find a durable spot on mineral soil or rock. A freestanding tent can come in handy on desert treks because many of the comfortable and durable campsites are located on smooth expanses of slickrock.

Campfires are generally inappropriate in desert environments due to the lack of downed wood. Even if you do find a scattering of juniper or cedar branches lying around, they are likely the irreplaceable homes of a variety of desert critters. Bring warm clothing and a camp stove, however, to keep yourself warm on chilly desert nights when the temperature drops dramatically from the daytime high.

Avoid disrupting wildlife and their access to the area's precious few water sources. Unless you are camped near a perennial stream or river, extract water from area sources *only* for drinking. A *tinaja*—a puddle of water in a rock depression—may not look like much to humans, but it is a wildlife oasis and can easily be depleted by one camping party.

Waste Disposal

Despite the fact that it was something of an LNT fad about five years ago, surface disposal of human waste is not advised in desert environments. Visitation to our nation's arid lands has increased so dramatically over the last decade that few people will find themselves in a location remote enough for smearing.

Cat holes are the preferred option in most desert landscapes. Keep in mind that your deposit will be there for a long time because decomposition is very slow; make sure the hole is at least 200 feet away from water sources or washes and gullies that could be filled with water after a rain.

No matter how sweaty you are, small water sources such as *tinajas* or springs are inappropriate to use for bathing. Even if you are not using soap, these precious few water sources can become easily polluted by human body oils and topical applications like sunscreen. Desert animals rely on these for drinking water, so do not use them for bathing.

LNT Basics: Tundra and Desert Travel
Travel on Durable Surfaces
- **Arctic tundra:** Whenever possible, hike on established trails. In the absence of established pathways, seek out boulder-strewn streambeds. If you find it necessary to travel across the tundra, try to walk on ground that is dry and covered with grasses or sedges rather than low shrubs or lichen beds.

- **Alpine tundra:** Stay on established trails and avoid "volunteer" paths. Wear gaiters—and crampons, if necessary—so you can walk through mud, snow, and ice on the trail rather than around it.
- **Desert:** Avoid stepping on cryptobiotic soil—black, clumpy groundcover that is self-sustaining biological communities. Hike on established trails. If you find yourself in a region without established trails, slickrock and gravel or sand washes are the most durable surfaces.

Making Camp

- **Arctic tundra:** If you have the option of camping at an established site, do so. The next best option is to camp in the gravel bed of a stream drainage or on exposed mineral soil in the fold of a hill.
- **Alpine tundra:** In general, places above tree line don't make ideal campsites. But if you find it necessary to pitch your tent above tree line, try to do it at an established site. When an established site isn't available, choose a resistant surface such as snow, rock, or mineral soil.
- **Desert:** Camp at established sites. If you find yourself in a region without established campsites, slickrock, gravel and sand are the most durable surfaces. (But don't camp in washes because of the danger of flash floods.)
- Because of the lack of downed wood, slow plant growth, and fragile soils, fires are inappropriate in most tundra and desert environments.

Conserve Water in the Desert

- Most desert hikers should carry at least one gallon per person per day.
- Avoid disrupting wildlife and their access to the area's scarce water sources. Unless you are camped near a perennial stream or river, extract water from area sources *ONLY* for drinking.
- Small water sources are inappropriate for bathing. Even if you are not using soap, these water sources can become easily polluted by humans.

Properly Dispose of Human Waste

- **Arctic tundra:** Smearing feces may be the best poop placement option; surface disposal should only be used if visitation to the region is very low and you are visiting the tundra environment during summer when there is plenty of sunlight to speed decomposition. If you are visiting a popular area in the Arctic, dispose of waste in a cat hole when possible.
- **Alpine tundra:** Even if it is not required, packing out poop may very likely be the best option. An alternative is to hike down to tree line or into a side canyon and find suitable soil for digging a cat hole.
- **Desert:** Cat holes are the preferred option in most desert landscapes. Make sure the hole is at least 200 feet away from water sources or washes and gullies that could be filled with water after a rain. Surface disposal is inappropriate except in extremely remote areas.

ARCHAEOLOGICAL AND HISTORICAL SITES

From Civil War battlefields on the East Coast to ancient Anasazi ruins on the Colorado Plateau to Indian petroglyphs in the Pacific Northwest, our nation's wildlands harbor many historic and prehistoric cultural treasures. Technically, these sites are protected under the Archaelogical Resources Protection Act of 1979 and the Antiquities Protection Act of 1906. It is a federal offense to disturb or destroy archaeological and historic sites, and many people have been sent to jail for doing so.

The problem, however, is that many of these sites are in remote backcountry areas, and illegal activity can occur virtually unmonitored. But an even bigger problem is that most damage inflicted on our nation's cultural treasures is done so unknowingly, by well-meaning wilderness travelers who just want to have a closer look.

The desert environments in the Southwest are especially vulnerable to vandalism of archaeological sites. The dramatic increase in backcountry visitation to public lands on the Colorado Plateau, combined with the concentration of archaeological sites in the region, for example, are making a delicate environment that much more vulnerable to human impacts.

"The ruins and rock art of the Southwest are being loved to death," noted Rick Moore of the nonprofit group Grand Canyon Trust. "It is difficult to convince people that seemingly innocent acts that have no perceptible impact can be severely damaging over time. The cumulative effect of a thousand light touches to a wall makes it fall apart."

Some of the destruction to archaeological sites in the Southwest is blatant vandalism, but most of it is due to what Moore called "innocent acts that destroy." The loss is great because many of the Indian ruins and rock art in the region date back to before Columbus set foot in America, and some date back to before Christ.

If you happen to be hiking and camping in an area where there are

Disturbing ancient Indian artifacts (even sticking a pottery sherd in your pocket) is against federal law. (photo courtesy of NOLS)

archaeological sites, follow these guidelines to keep these treasures preserved for future generations:

- As you approach an archaeological site, stop for a moment and think about how you can minimize your impact. Stay off the midden, which is usually a low mound near the site that is the original inhabitants' trash pile and holds valuable information for archaeologists.
- Stay on established trails around the site and avoid walking along the base of walls built on slopes. Erosion will make them topple.
- Walls that are stressed once too often can collapse. Do not use them as handholds to gain access to a site, and do not stand or climb on them.
- Try to camp at least 200 feet from archaeological sites.
- Do not pick up any artifact. If you do accidentally move something (like a potsherd), put it back exactly where you found it.
- Charcoal and soot remains are used to carbon-date sites. Modern charcoal and soot contaminate the ancient record, so do not build campfires near a site.
- Do not touch rock art; oils from human skin can cumulatively destroy the mineral-based paints.

These prehistoric Anasazi pictographs can be damaged by the human touch. (photo by Mike Frick)

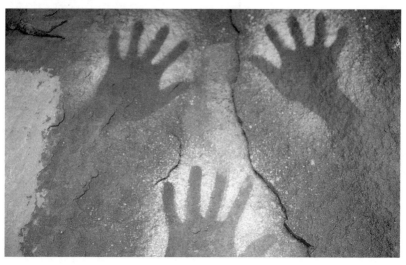

- Children's natural curiosity and enthusiasm for climbing can be aroused by the walls, nooks, and crannies found at most sites. Hold youngsters' hands while visiting, and explain to them the reasons for not exploring too vigorously.

In general, practice the LNT principle of "leave what you find." This applies everywhere—whether you are tempted to touch rock art in Canyonlands National Park, pick up a piece of petrified wood in the Painted Desert, or pocket a metal buckle lying on the ground at Gettysburg.

LNT Basics: Minimizing Impacts to Archaeological and Historical Sites

- As you approach an archaeological site, stay off the midden, usually a low mound near the site, which is the original inhabitants' trash pile and which holds valuable information for archaeologists.
- Stay on established trails around the site and avoid walking along the base of walls built on slopes. Erosion will make them topple.
- Walls that are stressed once too often can collapse. Do not use them as handholds to gain access to a site, and do not stand or climb on them.
- Try to camp at least 200 feet away from archaeological sites.
- Do not pick up any artifact. If you do accidentally move something (like a potsherd), put it back exactly where you found it.
- Charcoal and soot remains are used to date sites. The ancient record is contaminated by modern charcoal and soot, so do not build campfires near a site.
- Do not touch rock art; oils from human skin can cumulatively destroy the mineral-based paints.
- Hold youngsters' hands while visiting and explain to them why they should stay off the site.

CHAPTER 7

SHARING THE LNT MESSAGE

—

Teaching Minimum-Impact Techniques to Kids, Friends, and Strangers

IF YOUR HIKING PARTNER WAS BITTEN by a rattlesnake would you cut the wound and try to suck the venom out? Have you ever taken salt tablets in an effort to stay hydrated during strenuous activity? Would you give a shivering friend whisky to help warm him up?

Anyone who is familiar with wilderness medicine practices knows the answer to all these questions should be a hearty "no." Modern science has proven beyond a shadow of a doubt that these old-time folk remedies are the stuff of medical myth and will only make people feel worse.

But if you haven't been educated in first aid, and you grew up in an environment where people swore by these kinds of folk remedies, how would you know the "cut and suck" method only promotes infection in a snakebite victim? And if someone were to suddenly tell you that much of what you'd been taught about how to care for ailing people in the backcountry was wrong, you might not respond very favorably.

I view Leave No Trace as a kind of preventive medicine and first aid for the land. It requires knowledge of certain principles and learned skills to promote environmental health. People who know these skills are no better than the people who don't know them; they are just better informed. There is also a certain universal environmental ethic behind LNT, just as there is a humanitarian ethic behind wilderness medicine. Most people want to help protect the wilderness, not destroy it—just as they would want to assist an injured person they encounter along the trail.

In the majority of instances where human impacts are damaging wildlands, it is due to a lack of knowledge about how to protect the

Practicing the Leave No Trace ethic should be a family affair. Here, a group plans their hiking route. (photo courtesy of NOLS)

health of these special places rather than maliciousness. Many people still don't know that the traditional camping and backcountry travel practices used for generations damage the environment. And because there are so many more wildland visitors hitting the trail every weekend than there are land managers available to counsel them, it is highly unlikely that these people will change their high-impact ways based on a chance encounter with a ranger.

The future success of Leave No Trace—and of wildlands preservation in general—depends on education, and on the ability of backcountry users to educate each other in the new wilderness etiquette. The best place to begin this education, of course, is in the home, with your family. Now that you've read this book, hopefully, you have become knowledgeable in Leave No Trace skills and have the desire to share that knowledge with others. What follows are some suggestions on how to educate your children, your friends, and even strangers you may meet on the trail about minimum-impact techniques.

TEACHING LNT PRACTICES TO KIDS

It was not too long ago that the *Boy Scout Handbook* offered detailed information on how to disturb and destroy the wilderness landscape. That was not the authors' intention, of course, but standard camping practices in the 1960s and before—including those of the Boy Scouts— were inevitably high-impact.

Children were taught that if they wanted to be good campers, they needed to dig a trench around their tent, cut down tree boughs for a bed, build a big campfire, and bury their trash when they vacated the site. Those young campers grew up to be big campers, and the Leave No Trace program has been reaching out to these people in an effort to teach them more environmentally responsible camping practices.

In addition to helping longtime wilderness users learn new camping tricks, a major component of the Leave No Trace program is aimed at teaching children proper minimum-impact skills from the start. Today, the *Boy Scout Handbook* offers detailed information on how to practice the principles of Leave No Trace, and all those circa-1960s high-impact campcraft skills are considered ancient history. In fact, the Leave No Trace ethic has become an important part of the Boy

Children on a sea kayaking trip can have lots of LNT fun, including making sand sculptures. (photo © Dorcas Miller)

Scout philosophy, and efforts are underway across the country to teach everyone from troop leaders to young Cub Scouts the latest in environmental responsibility and minimum-impact techniques.

Along with the Boy Scouts of America, many other outdoor organizations and land management offices have taken on the charge of teaching the new wilderness etiquette to children. Conservation-minded adults recognize that the future prospects for protecting wildlands through Leave No Trace ethics are only as good as the minimum-impact skills of our future wilderness users—today's children.

LNT practices are being taught to children through three primary venues: schools, youth-oriented outdoor programs, and family role models, including parents, siblings, and relatives. If you are working with children in a group setting and want to teach them LNT principles or you would just like to inspire your own child with a minimum-impact ethic, keep in mind the following:

Kids like to do things: A child's world is full of discovery, and learning about nature and LNT practices should be an active process. Contests and games are effective teaching methods. Also, introduce an element of excitement into the activity whenever possible. For example, go for a walk at night and listen for owls. See who can wash dishes with the least amount of water. March through the mud on a trail, rather than around it.

Tell stories, do not preach: There is no better way to lose the attention of children than to lecture them. If you are not teaching them through an activity, then make it into a story. For example, if you want a child to understand why he or she should not throw food scraps on the ground, tell him or her a tale about a mother fox and her kits who learned to live off garbage instead of hunting for their dinner. When the garbage was gone, the fox family went hungry because they did not know how to hunt.

Look for "teachable moments": If you are in the backcountry, you will likely encounter many situations along the way that illustrate Leave No Trace principles. Being able to point out trail erosion, for example, and showing the lack of vegetation around the disturbed area is a much more effective way to teach the "travel on durable surfaces" principle than just hypothetically explaining it.

Have fun: According to John Gookin, NOLS curriculum manager, it is important not to take things too seriously. "If I had cautionary advice," he said in an LNT newsletter article, "it would be to carefully balance and integrate the learning with fun, and especially raw adventure. Kids do not want to waste their time learning to pass some written test; they want to learn cool stuff that their friends will think is neat."

Help kids feel connected to nature: Because most children grow up in a relatively urban environment, the undeveloped backcountry can seem like a very foreign place. In order for a child to understand why nature should be protected, he or she needs to feel connected to it. When hiking, point out how a tree has skin just like we do. When drinking tap water at home, explain that it comes from rivers and lakes in places you may have visited, and keeping those places clean helps keep our drinking water clean. Peek in a fallen log and show your child how insects need to have a roof over their heads just like people do.

The LNT program offers a variety of guidance materials for teaching children minimum-impact skills and ethics. Below is a look at some successful LNT education initiatives being used around the country, and some additional suggestions on effective ways to teach our future wilderness users how to preserve the land.

This sign in Zion National Park indicates the trail is closed to allow the area to recover from hiker trampling. (photo by Annette McGivney)

▲ ▲ ▲

The LNT Song
From Scouting Ahead
(Sung to the tune of "Row, Row, Row Your Boat")

Sack, sack, sack your trash,
Put it in a bag.
Pack it out on your back,
Cause leaving it's a drag.

Sniff, sniff, sniff the flowers,
Leave them where they grow.
Endangered plants you pick today
Your kids may never know.

Camp, camp far away
From the fragile shore,
And when you do you'll save the lake.
It's clean water we're working for.

Cook, cook, cook your food
On a backpack stove.
Save the snags and save the trees
Cause wilderness is gold.

Dig, dig, dig a hole
About six inches down;
When nature calls, bury your waste
And leave it underground.

Leave, leave, leave no trace
With your camping gear,
Cause no one, no one in the woods
Wants to see you've been here.

Think, plan, and be aware
In nature's fragile place.
In wilderness we're visitors;
Protect this unspoiled space.

Schools: Bringing Conservation to the Classroom

He is a gruesome sight—a blaring boom box on his shoulder, a cigarette hanging out of his mouth, vandalizing trail signs and tormenting wildlife. The "Impact Monster" is a character used in skits to show schoolchildren what is meant, exactly, by bad behavior from an LNT standpoint.

Many Forest Service districts across the United States are performing "Impact Monster" skits in local elementary schools to teach young children the basics of Leave No Trace. Skits vary from district to district, but the memorable Barney-gone-bad character is always "noisy, gross, and sloppy." For example, in the skit as performed by the Tonto National Forest's Mesa Ranger District in Mesa, Arizona, the "Impact Monster" throws cigarette butts on the ground, carves graffiti into trail signs, and wraps toilet paper around a saguaro cactus.

According to Tonto National Forest staff member Greg Hansen, who has been teaching the LNT message at Mesa schools for fifteen years, the "Impact Monster" skit is most effective with fourth-graders. Willing rangers from the national forest also regularly appear at Mesa area schools to perform a "Woodsy Owl" skit for second-graders and a "Web of Life" ecology program for third-graders, and to promote a Junior Ranger program for older kids.

Like Forest Service youth outreach efforts around the country, the programs developed by Tonto National Forest staff are aimed at teaching children about wilderness preservation and minimum-impact skills before they ever hit the trail. "We concentrate on our future users," said Hansen in a recent conversation. "Our strategy is to make the educational effort progressive, so the kids keep learning new things every year."

Hansen added that, when teaching children about Leave No Trace, the kids have to be able to relate to the message or it will not hit home. For example, instead of saying it is bad to use soap when washing in a spring because it hurts plant and animal life, they illustrate the principle graphically. "We take a glass of water and pour dishsoap in it," explained Hansen. "Then we hold out the glass and ask the kids if they would drink from it."

In addition to the skits and programs offered to schools by the Forest Service and other land management agencies, the LNT program is also working its way into school curricula. A popular tool used by teachers to illustrate LNT principles and environmental conservation is the "Wilderness Box." Inside this large plastic container are various tools of the LNT trade: a trowel, a fire pan, posters containing LNT principles, animal bones, et cetera. The teachers are given a syllabus and encouraged to incorporate the curriculum into lesson plans for various subjects instead of trying to deliver the entire LNT message in one "environmental education" class. Overall, those involved in teaching Leave No Trace to schoolchildren say the efforts are most effective when the program is interactive and hands-on.

To get information and materials on the "Impact Monster" skit, the "Wilderness Box," or other educational programs for schools, contact the LNT office in Lander, Wyoming (see the appendix).

Outdoor Organizations: The Scoop on the Troops

Leave No Trace principles have been incorporated into Boy Scout education programs on many different levels. Troop leaders, for example, are trained by LNT staff during an annual workshop at the Philmont Training Center in New Mexico. Thousands of boys each year learn about LNT through the minimum-impact skills camp at

Philmont Scout Ranch. However, one of the most impressive efforts to spread the LNT gospel to young wilderness users is the Scouting Ahead program.

Scouting Ahead is a cooperative effort formed five years ago by Boy Scouts of America, Girl Scouts of the Puget Sound Area, the Washington Wilderness Coalition, The Mountaineers, and the U.S. Forest Service. Scouting Ahead was conceived in an effort to teach minimum-impact skills to children and help preserve wilderness areas in the Pacific Northwest. Since its inception, more than 400 troop leaders and 8,000 scouts have participated in the program. Scouting Ahead is composed of three primary program components:

The Scouting Ahead workshop: Held annually, the workshop trains troop leaders in minimum-impact skills and LNT ethics. The leaders are given a detailed Scouting Ahead manual and coached on how to teach the material to children.

Troop training: Once the leader has completed the workshop and "accepts the LNT challenge," he or she is charged with training the troop. The *Scouting Ahead* manual provides techniques and activities for teaching Leave No Trace principles. Teaching methods include hypothetical problem solving—such as deciding which is the most durable surface on which to camp—and hands-on exercises in, for example, cooking on a small camp stove and learning how to dehydrate foods.

Leave No Trace certification: This annual event is the highlight of the Scouting Ahead program. Both troop leaders and scouts are tested in minimum-impact skills, and those who pass are awarded an LNT merit badge. The daylong certification process involves a written exam and field exercises.

According to Adrienne Hall of the Mount Baker–Snoqualmie National Forest, which hosts the LNT certification, the field exercises are rigorous and by the end of the day, most kids are "pretty burned out." In a recent conversation, she said the scouts are tested in numerous field demonstrations: they must pick the "ten essentials" to put in their backpack, cook a meal and properly dispose of food wastes, pick the proper campsite, take a break along the trail the LNT way, and hike through snow without eroding the trail. "Hands-on activities are by far the most popular way for the scouts to learn about Leave No Trace," she said.

A Family Affair: Teaching Your Child LNT Values

The bottom line for teaching children Leave No Trace skills and ethics is that it should start in the home. The minimum-impact approach to wilderness travel is, in a larger sense, an approach to living (see Adopting an LNT Lifestyle at the end of this chapter), and something that is most logically handed down to a child from his or her parents.

If you want to instill your child with a working knowledge of the new wilderness etiquette, keep in mind that kids (especially young ones) like action. When going on backcountry outings, incorporate activities that will help teach your child LNT principles and spice up the experience. Here are some suggestions:

- When camping, sit by the light of your flashlight covered with a red bandana and try to identify constellations. Help your child become accustomed to spending nights in the backcountry without the glow of a campfire.

- When hiking, equip each family member with a small plastic bag and have a contest to see who can pick up the most trash. Point out to your child all the "micro-trash" along the trail, like cigarette butts, food bar wrappers, and even fuzz balls. Make sure he or she understands, however, not to pick up toilet paper. You can tell your child how "icky" and inconsiderate it is for someone to leave something so full of germs in such a beautiful place.

- When hiking, have a contest to see who can spot the most birds and animals along the way. This will help your child understand how many creatures live in the backcountry and depend on a clean environment.

- When backpacking, let your child choose the campsite, relying on his or her knowledge of LNT criteria. Write down on an index card what an established site looks like (see LNT Basics: Choosing a Campsite in chapter 1, All About Camping). After you have set up camp, wander around and see if your child can find a campsite in which impact is just beginning, so that the campsite should not be used if it can be avoided.

- Involve your child in food planning and preparation. Take him or her with you to the grocery store to buy ingredients for one-pot meals that will lighten the load in the backpack, require less water, and require less cleanup. Pasta, beans, or couscous are good choices. Make cooking and cleanup a family affair.
- When in camp, play a game in which your children close their eyes and try to guess what an item is just by smelling it—soap, a tea bag, gorp. Then explain that animals are strongly guided by their sense of smell, and these odors will draw them into camp if the items are left out.
- Call your local Forest Service office and see if you and your child can go on a patrol or hike with a wilderness ranger. This is an excellent way for your child to visit the front line in the war against human impacts on public lands. Both you and your child will likely be interested in learning about what kinds of environmental issues a ranger deals with.
- Involve your child in a local trail cleanup. Hiking clubs and Forest Service ranger districts frequently hold volunteer trail maintenance activities. Make sure the trail work is simple (like picking up trash) and suitable for a child. To find out about trail projects in your area, call local land management offices or inquire at an outdoor retailer about local hiking clubs (see the appendix for some ideas).

In the end, of course, there is no more effective method of teaching your child about what is important than through your own example. Chances are that if you live by an LNT ethic and strive to minimize impacts wherever you go, so will your child. And when he or she grows up, your child will pass the philosophy on to his or her children who, hopefully, will have as much wilderness to enjoy as we do.

LNT Basics: Tips for Teaching Kids LNT Practices
- **Kids like to do things:** Learning about nature and LNT practices should be an active process. Contests and games are effective teaching methods, as is anything that incorporates an element of excitement.

- **Tell stories, do not preach:** If what you are teaching is not through an activity, then make it into a story.
- **Look for "teachable moments":** In the backcountry, you will likely encounter many situations that illustrate Leave No Trace principles. Point out a real-life example of some LNT technique.
- **Have fun:** Carefully balance and integrate learning with fun, and especially raw adventure.
- **Help kids feel connected to nature:** When visiting the backcountry, point out common characteristics between the child and the undeveloped surroundings.

TEACHING LNT PRACTICES TO GROWN-UPS

What follows are some suggestions on how to educate both your friends and strangers you may meet on the trail in minimum-impact techniques.

Teach, do not preach: Think of Leave No Trace as a set of skills that are learned, like modern first-aid practices. There is no moral high ground that must be taken in order to impart knowledge about basic things like backcountry waste disposal or trail erosion. People—especially strangers—are instantly turned off by ethical arguments; just stick with the tangible facts.

Show them "a better way": Never be condescending by telling a person they are doing something "wrong." Remember, if they are in the backcountry, they are likely there because they enjoy the place as much as you do and do not want to damage it. In communicating the Leave No Trace message, land managers discovered early on that the most effective approach for instructing people was to offer to show them "a better way." In other words, if a party has their horses tied to trees, it is not "the wrong way," but you can show them "a better way" to restrain their animals that will not damage vegetation.

Emphasize the "authority of the resource": When wilderness rangers are trained at the Arthur Carhart National Training Center in Montana, they are taught to influence visitor behavior through the "authority of the resource" instead of through the perceived authority that comes with the badge and/or gun they wear. In other words,

When explaining land management regulations to their students, NOLS instructors try to emphasize the "authority of the resource." (photo courtesy of NOLS)

encourage people to change their behavior based on their desire to help the environment rather than to obey an authority figure.

"Wilderness areas are among the few places on earth where we have agreed to allow nature, for the most part, to operate on its own terms," says the ranger training manual. "Desirable behavior is more likely to occur if people understand how their actions affect the way nature operates."

If you are just another hiker rather than a law enforcer, emphasizing the "authority of the resource" is even more important because it is unlikely that people are going to change their behavior just because you say they should. When utilizing the "authority of the resource" technique, focus on environmental impacts rather than rules and regulations. For example, if you encounter a party that is having a campfire in an area where fires are banned, explain to them how fires damage soils and strip the land of fallen wood, an essential ingredient to a healthy ecosystem. Then, after the fact, you can throw in that campfires also happen to be against the rules and they could be fined if caught.

WHAT TO DO WHEN...

Saying we should all become LNT evangelists and spread the minimum-impact gospel is one thing, but actually doing it is another. If you encounter a well-armed hunting party in the woods sitting around a big fire drinking beer, is it a good idea to share with them why campfires are harmful to the environment? Sometimes the situation will not be right for sharing the minimum-impact message. Knowing when and how to approach strangers about Leave No Trace principles can be difficult—and, sometimes, approaching friends can be even tougher. Of course, you will have to rely on your own good judgment in deciding when the time is right to teach LNT practices; personal safety should never be compromised. However, here are a few hypothetical scenarios that may help guide you in your evangelical endeavors.

Campfires

Situation: You are on a canoe trip with a group of friends. In camp, they want to build a nice, warm blaze in the fire ring, so they begin scavenging the area for big pieces of wood.

Recommended action: Be an LNT realist. It is unlikely that this group can be convinced they should go cold turkey on the campfire idea. You can explain to them why it is best, from an environmental standpoint, to rely just on a camp stove and not to have a campfire at all. But, then you can suggest that if they would still like to have fire, there are techniques you can show them that will not damage the soil at the campsite or deplete the area of ecologically important fallen logs. Because it is unlikely that anyone has brought along a fire pan, show them how to build a mound fire (see How to Build a Fire the LNT Way in chapter 1, All About Camping). Demonstrate that a cozy blaze can be made using small twigs rather than big logs.

If you want to have a campfire, building a mound fire is usually the path of least resistance. (photo courtesy of NOLS)

Shortcuts
Situation: You are hiking up a steep summit trail toward a mountain peak, and a group of adolescents on a school field trip appears from below after shortcutting up the switchback. They are in a race to the summit and continue pioneering their direct route to the top, disregarding the established trail.

Recommended action: Stop the children and ask them to look at the eroded "volunteer" that they have just hiked up. Point out that there is no vegetation on or around the path compared to other areas away from the trail. Tell them that the alpine environment is very fragile and when they hike off the main trail, they are destroying nutrients that plants and animals must have in order to live. Also, try to find the group's leader and explain to him or her what you have also explained to the children.

Archaeological Sites
Situation: You are backpacking in a remote section of a national park in southern Utah and you encounter a truck that is backed up to an

alcove where there are Indian ruins. There are several people in the alcove and they appear to be digging.

Recommended action: You have likely stumbled upon "pot hunters" who make their living by stealing valuable artifacts from federally owned archaeological sites. They are knowingly breaking the law (violating the Archaeological Resources Protection Act, and driving a motorized vehicle into a wilderness area) and may very well be armed. Do not jeopardize your safety by imparting the "leave what you find" LNT principle to these scoundrels. As inconspicuously as possible, take note of the license plate number and a general description of the people (how many, clothing, et cetera), and hike back to the land management office or find a ranger as soon as possible. Tell them what you saw and let those in charge of enforcing the law deal with the looters. In most vandalism cases, you will run across people who just do not know any better and are ripe for LNT education. But do not be naive enough to assume that everyone is acting out of ignorance.

Mountain Bikers

Situation: You are horseback riding in a federal wilderness area and encounter a mountain biker speeding down the trail.

Recommended action: There is understandable cause for anger here because the mountain biker is not only breaking the law by being in a wilderness area, but he or she could have spooked your horse and caused an accident. Anger, however, gets you nowhere in educating this wayward biker about minimizing impacts.

Be optimistic and assume that the mountain biker does not know that he or she is in a wilderness area or that bikes are not allowed in wilderness areas. Ask the biker if he or she is familiar with the federal Wilderness Act (see A Return to the Wilderness in the Introduction). Explain that he or she is in an area set aside for preservation under the Wilderness Act and it is off-limits to all mechanized vehicles, including mountain bikes. Then add that his or her speeding bike could have startled your horse and both of you could have been injured. Hopefully, the mountain biker will apologize and backtrack out of the wilderness. But if he or she ignores your advice and keeps riding, report the encounter to the land management office when you return to the trailhead.

ADOPTING AN LNT LIFESTYLE

The new wilderness etiquette outlined in this book is not intended to be something you practice only when you are in the backcountry. Although the Leave No Trace program was designed to specifically address visitor impacts in wildland areas, the ethic behind the six basic LNT principles can be applied to all aspects of your life—in the office, at home, in the city park, as well as on outings in the backcountry.

Living in a way in which we strive to minimize impacts on the environment should involve all types of conservation practices, such as recycling, composting, conserving water, and using public transportation. Even if we never set foot in wilderness areas, a consumptive life in the city is ultimately going to affect those "pristine" places, whether it

This LNT Master's course graduate is full of enthusiasm for making the wilderness a cleaner place. (photo courtesy of NOLS)

is through air pollution, depleting the water table, or an insatiable need for timber to build houses.

As we enter the twenty-first century, two things are certain: the number of people in the United States will continue to grow, and the amount of wilderness in this country will either stay the same or decrease. Consequently, if we are to preserve what wildlands we have left, we will either have to essentially ban human visitors from the protected areas, or we can make LNT practices so pervasive among backcountry users that the prospect of "loving the wilderness to death" is no longer a threat to the environment.

The choice seems simple—especially when you think of it in the way conservationist and author Aldo Leopold viewed humankind's relationship to wilderness. "Man always kills the thing he loves, and so we the pioneers have killed our wilderness," wrote Leopold in *A Sand County Almanac.* "Some say we had to. Be that as it may, I am glad I shall never be young without wild country to be young in. Of what avail are forty freedoms without a blank spot on the map?"

LNT Basics: Tips for Teaching Adult LNT Practices

- **Teach, do not preach:** Think of Leave No Trace as a set of skills that are learned, like modern first-aid practices. There is no moral high ground that must be taken in order to impart knowledge about basic things like backcountry waste disposal or trail erosion.
- **Show them "a better way":** Never be condescending by telling a person they are doing something "wrong." In communicating the Leave No Trace message, offer to show them "a better way" rather than condemn their environmentally harmful actions.
- **Emphasize the "authority of the resource":** Encourage people to change their behavior based on their desire to help the environment rather than the need to obey an authority figure. When utilizing the "authority of the resource"

technique, focus on environmental impacts, not rules and regulations.

- Make your life at home an example of the LNT ethic: Strive to minimize impacts on the environment through conservation practices such as recycling, composting, conserving water, and using public transportation. Even if we never set foot in wilderness areas, a consumptive life in the city is ultimately going to affect those "pristine" places.

Appendix: LNT Resources

The Access Fund (LNT information for climbers)
   P.O. Box 17010
   Boulder, CO 80308
   (303) 545-6772

American Hiking Society
   P.O. Box 20160
   Washington, DC 20041
   (703) 385-3252

Backcountry Horsemen of America
   P.O. Box 1192
   Columbia Falls, MT 59912

Bureau of Land Management LNT Coordinator, Stew Jacobsen
   BLM, Utah State Office
   324 South State Street
   Salt Lake City, UT 84111
   (801) 539-4235

The Grand Canyon Trust (protection of Southwest archaeological
   resources)
   Route 4, Box 718
   Flagstaff, AZ 86001
   (520) 774-7488

International Mountain Biking Association
   P.O. Box 7578
   Boulder, CO 80306
   (303) 545-9011

Leave No Trace, Inc. (materials and information)
P.O. Box 997
Boulder, CO 80306
(303) 442-8222; (800) 332-4100
http://www.lnt.org

Maine Island Trail Association (support for management of Maine
Island Trail)
P.O. Box C
Rockland, Maine 04841
(207) 596-6456

National Outdoor Leadership School (NOLS) Outreach
288 Main Street
Lander, WY 82520
(307) 332-1282

National Park Service LNT Coordinator, Rogue Selmer
Glacier National Park
P.O. Box 128
West Glacier, MT 59936
(406) 888-7800

Scouting Ahead (training program for Boy Scouts and troop leaders)
c/o Washington Wilderness Coalition
4649 Sunnyside Avenue North
Seattle, WA 98105
(206) 633-1992

U.S. Forest Service LNT Office, Ralph Swain
20235 Remont Road
Huson, MT 59846
(406) 622-5208

Recommended Reading

Abbey, Edward. *Desert Solitaire*. New York: Ballantine Books, 1968.

Cole, David, and William Hammitt. *Wildland Recreation: Ecology and Management*. New York: John Wiley & Sons, 1987.

Cole, David, and Bruce Hampton. *Soft Paths*. Mechanicsburg, Penn.: NOLS/Stackpole Books, 1995.

Foreman, Dave, and Howie Wolke. *The Big Outside: A Descriptive Inventory of Big Wilderness Areas in the United States*. New York: Harmony Books, 1992.

Leopold, Aldo. *A Sand County Almanac*. New York: Ballantine Books, 1970.

Meyer, Kathleen. *How to Shit in the Woods*. Berkeley, Calif.: Ten Speed Press, 1994.

Nash, Roderick. *Wilderness and the American Mind*. New Haven, Conn.: Yale University Press, 1982.

National Outdoor Leadership School. "Alaskan Tundra." "Backcountry Horse Use." "Desert and Canyon Country." "Pacific Northwest." "Rock Climbing." "North America." "Northeast Mountains." "Rocky Mountains." "Sierra Nevada." "Southeastern States." "Temperate Coastal Zones." "Western River Corridors." All in *LNT Skills and Ethics Series, Sierra Nevada* 120 (July 1997).

References

Introduction

Alt, Tom. Telephone conversation with author, August 1996.

Brame, Susan Chadwick, and Chad Henderson. *An Introduction to Wildland Ethics and Management*, p. 79. Lander, Wyo.: National Outdoor Leadership School, 1992.

Cole, David. "The Changing Wilderness." Leave No Trace Program *Master Network* newsletter no. 8 (fall 1994).

———.Telephone conversation with author, July 1996.

———. *Wilderness Recreation Use Trends, 1965–1994*, p. 3. Ogden, Utah: USFS Intermountain Research Station, 1996.

Cole, David, and Beth Ranz. "Temporary Campsite Closures in the Selway-Bitterroot Wilderness. *Journal of Forestry* 81, no. 11 (November 1983): pp. 729–32.

Library of Congress. Statutes at Large. website address: LCWeb.loc.gov. U.S. Code, Title 16, Chapter 23. The Wilderness Act of Sept. 3, 1964.

Nash, Roderick. *Wilderness and the American Mind*. New Haven, Conn.: Yale University Press, 1982.

National Outdoor Leadership School. "Low-Impact Use of Arid Land Environments: A Bureau of Land Management Training Opportunity," p. 57. Presented by NOLS at Clover Mountains Wilderness Study Area, March 1995.

Spencer, Edward L., Herbert E. Echelberger, Raymond E. Leonard, and Craig Evans. "Trends in Hiking and Backcountry Use," pp. 195–98. In *Proceedings, 1980 National Outdoor Recreation Trends Symposium*, Wilbur F. LaPage, ed. U.S. Department of Agriculture, Forest Service, Northeast Forest Experiment Station, 1980.

Thompson, Bill. Telephone conversation with author, October 1996.

U.S. Forest Service. *Proceedings of the Second Symposium on Social Aspects and Recreation Research*, Pacific Southwest Research Station, February 23–25, 1994.

Wyant, William K. *Westward in Eden: The Public Lands and the Conservation Movement*, pp. 12–13. Berkeley, Calif.: University of California Press, 1978.

Chapter 1

Cole, David. "Backcountry Impact Management: Lessons from Research." *Backcountry Recreation Management Trends* 31, no. 3 (1994): pp. 10–14.

———. *Campsites in Three Western Wildernesses: Proliferation and Changes in Condition Over 12 to 16 Years*. Ogden, Utah: U.S. Department of Agriculture, Forest Service, Intermountain Research Station, 1993.

———. *Monitoring the Conditions of Wilderness Campsites*. Ogden, Utah: U.S. Department of Agriculture, Forest Service, Intermountain Research Station, 1983.

Cole, David, and William Hammitt. *Wildland Recreation: Ecology and Management*. New York: John Wiley & Sons, 1987.

Hart, John. *Walking Softly in the Wilderness*. San Francisco, Calif.: Sierra Club Books, 1984.

Marion, Jeffrey. *Results from the Application of a Campsite Inventory and Impact Monitoring System in Eleven Wilderness Areas of the Jefferson National Forest*. Blacksburg, Va.: National Park Service, Cooperative Park Studies Unit, Virginia Tech, 1991.

Marion, Jeff, David Cole, and David Reynolds. "Limits of Acceptable Change: A Framework for Assessing Carrying Capacity." *Park Science*, National Park Service (fall 1985).

Marion, Jeff, Joseph Roggenbuck, and Robert Manning. *Problems and Practices in Backcountry Recreation Management: A Survey of National Park Service Managers*. Blacksburg, Virg.: National Park Service, Cooperative Park Studies Unit, Virginia Tech, 1993.

Monz, Chris. Interview with author, Lander, Wyoming, October 1996.

Smith, Del. Interview with author, Zion National Park, Utah, November 1996.

Chapter 2

BACKPACKER magazine. "Talking Dirty." *BACKPACKER* 22 (May 1994).

Brame, Rich. Interview with author, Lander, Wyoming, October 1996.

Cairncross, S. Control of Enteric Pathogens in Developing Countries. Pages 157-189 in R. Mitchell, ed. *Environmental Microbiology*. Wiley-Liss, Inc. New York.Washington, D.C.: World Health Organization, Regional Office for the Americas, 1992.

Holmes, Daniel. "Experiments on the Effects of Human Urine and Trampling on Subalpine Plants," p. 79. Berkeley, Calif.: University of California, Department of Geography, 1979.

Leemon, Dree. Correspondence with author, April 1997.

Meyer, Kathleen. *How to Shit in the Woods*. Berkeley, Calif.: Ten Speed Press, 1994.

Monz, Chris. Interview with author, Lander, Wyoming, October 1996.

National Park Service Organic Act of 1916. U.S. Code. Vol. 43, secs. 1–410 (March 2, 1917).

Reeves, Harry. "Human Waste Disposal in the Sierran Wilderness." In *A Report on the Wilderness Impact Study*, p. 140. San Francisco: Sierra Club, 1979.

Sawyer, Marit. Correspondence with author, April 1997.

Temple, Kenneth L., Anne K. Camper, and Robert C. Lucas. "Potential Health Hazard from Human Wastes in Wilderness." *Journal of Soil and Water Conservation* 37, no. 6 (November-December 1982): pp. 357–59.

Chapters 3, 4, and 5

Blumenthal, Tim. Telephone conversation with author, November 1996.

Bricler, S., B. Tunnicliff, and J. Utter. "Use and Quality of Wildland

Water: The Case of the Colorado River Corridor in the Grand Canyon." *Western Wildlands* 9 (1983): pp. 20–25.

Cole, David, and Mitchell McClaran. *Packstock in Wilderness: Use Impacts, Monitoring and Management*, p. 3. Ogden, Utah: U.S. Department of Agriculture, Forest Service, Intermountain Research Station, 1993.

Crumbo, Kim. Telephone conversation with author, December 1996.

Magnuson, Mark. "Grand Teton National Park Sees Changes in Climbing." Leave No Trace Program *Master Network* newsletter 9 (winter 1995).

Marion, Jeffrey. *An Assessment of Trail Conditions in Great Smoky Mountains National Park*, p. 127. Blacksburg, Virg.: U.S. Department of Interior, National Park Service, Southeast Region, 1993.

Mink, Virgil. Telephone conversation with author, September 1997.

Moser, Sally. Telephone conversation with author, November 1996.

National Sporting Goods Association. *The Sporting Goods Market in 1996*. Orlando, Fla.: National Sporting Goods Association, 1995.

Outdoor Recreation Coalition of America. *State of the Industry Report*. Boulder, Colo.: Outdoor Recreation Coalition of America, 1995.

Quarrier, Sid. Telephone conversation with author, December 1996.

Willard, B.E., and Marr, J.W. 1971. "Recovery of alpine tundra under protection after damage by human activities in the Rocky Mountains of Colorado." *Biological Conservation* (1971) 1:31:181-190.

Wilson, John, and Joseph Seney. "Erosional Impact of Hikers, Horses, Motorcycles, and Off-Road Bicycles on Mountain Trails in Montana." *Mountain Research and Development* 14, no. 1 (1994): pp. 77–88.

Chapter 6
Cole, David, and Bruce Hampton. *Soft Paths*. Mechanicsburg, Penn.: NOLS/Stackpole Books, 1995.

Cooper, D. J. "The Arrigetch Peaks Region of the Central Brooks Range, Alaska: Ecosystems and Human Use," *Proceedings, National Wilderness Conference Current Research*, pp. 94–99. Ogden, Utah: U.S. Department of Agriculture, Forest Service General Technical Report, Intermountain Research Station, 1985.

Ganci, Dave. *Desert Hiking*. Berkeley, Calif.: Wilderness Press, 1993.

Library of Congress. Statutes at Large. http://www.loc.gov/

Miller, Debbie S. *Midnight Wilderness: Journeys in Alaska's Arctic National Wildlife Refuge*. San Francisco: Sierra Club Books, 1990.

Moore, Rick. *Preserving Traces of the Past: Protecting the Colorado Plateau's Archaeological Heritage*. Flagstaff, Ariz.: The Grand Canyon Trust, 1994.

Chapter 7

Boy Scouts of America. *The Boy Scout Handbook: Trail to Eagle*. Irving, Texas: Boy Scouts of America, 1990.

Gookin, John. "Empowering Children with Active Learning Techniques." Leave No Trace Program *Master Network* newsletter 6 (winter 1994).

Hall, Adrienne. Telephone conversation with author, August 1997.

Hansen, Greg. Telephone conversation with author, August 1997.

Leave No Trace, Inc. *Teaching Leave No Trace: Activities for Teaching Responsible Outdoor Skills*. Boulder, Colo.: Leave No Trace, Inc., 1996.

Leopold, Aldo. *A Sand County Almanac*. New York: Ballantine Books, 1970.

Sawyer, Marit, ed. *Scouting Ahead*. 3d ed. Seattle: Washington Wilderness Coalition, 1996.

The Wilderness Ranger Training Manual, USDA Forest Service, Arthur Carhart National Wilderness Training Center, Helena, Montana. 1995.

Index

packing out, 23, 54-56, 57, 89-90, 93, 142, 160, 164
See also camp kitchen; waste disposal, human
trees, minimizing impact on
confining horses, 113-14, 117, 166
fuels for campfires, 44-45, 46, 56, 95, 96

U.S. Fish and Wildlife Service, 12
national wildlife refuges, 135-36
U.S. Forest Service, 12, 175
Leave No Trace education programs, 17-18, 24, 161-62, 163-64, 165
managing timber (logging) and trails (recreation), 35-36, 40
wilderness recreation impact studies, 15-16, 24, 32-33, 109
U.S. public lands, legislation
enforcement, 170
Federal Land Policy and Management Act (1976), 136-37
Forest Reserve Act (1891), 27, 35
Homestead Act (1862), 26
national monuments, 27-28
Wilderness Act, 6-7, 13-15, 83, 102, 137, 170
See also archaeological and historical sites, legislation
U.S. public lands, management
history of, 25-27
inventory of, 14-15
Leave No Trace ethic/education, 17-21
waste disposal, 61-65
See also archaeological and historical sites; national forests/wilderness areas; national monuments; national parks; national wildlife refuges; Eastern U.S. public lands; Southwestern U.S. public lands; Western U.S. public lands
Utah public lands
Canyonlands National Park, 41, 146, 153
deserts, 135, 144
Grand Staircase-Escalante National Monument, 137

Uinta Mountains, 18
wilderness designation, 15
Zion National Park, 70, 90, 146

vegetation, minimizing impact on, 159, 160
in alpine tundra, 140-42
in arctic tundra, 137-39
in deserts, 144-46
lichen beds, 123, 138-39, 148
on rock, 93, 94

waste disposal, animal
dog feces, 79-80
horse feces, 99, 108-09, 115, 117
waste disposal, human, 59, 67, 75-77
in alpine tundra, 142-43, 150
in arctic tundra, 69, 140, 150
cat holes, 21, 23, 60-61, 62, 66, 67-68, 69, 75-76, 90, 93, 130, 133, 140, 143, 148, 150, 160
decomposition, 59-61, 62, 67, 69, 75
deodorizers, 73
in deserts, 69, 148-50
diapers, 74, 76
feces, 58-64, 66-70, 71-73, 90, 93-94, 96, 115, 140, 150
latrines, 59-60, 62, 67, 68-69, 76
packing out, 70, 90, 93-94, 96, 123-24, 126, 130-32, 133, 140, 143, 150
poop tube, 70, 90, 94, 123-24, 126
portable toilets, 69, 70, 115, 130, 131-32, 133
on river trips, 119, 130-32, 133
for rock-climbers, 88-89, 90, 93-94
for sea kayakers, 119, 123-24, 126
"shit put," 67
smearing, 67, 69-70, 90, 140, 142-43, 148, 150
tampons/menstruation, 73, 76
toilet paper and alternatives, 23, 59, 66, 70-73, 74, 76, 164
toilets and outhouses, 62-63, 66, 69, 75, 90, 93
urine, 61, 62, 74, 96, 132, 133
winter camping, 96
water source
contamination, 61, 64, 67, 70, 74, 148

About the Author

A field editor for *BACKPACKER* magazine, Annette McGivney has been writing about environmental and wilderness preservation issues for nearly two decades. She is co-author of *Southwest Camping*, former editor of *Arizona Adventure* magazine and former managing editor of Rodale's *Guide to Family Camping*. Annette is a longtime backpacker who enjoys exploring the wilderness with her husband, Mike, and one-year-old son, Austin. She resides in Flagstaff, Arizona.

The mission of *BACKPACKER* magazine is to distribute, in a variety of media, credible, in-depth, and compelling "how-to-do-it" information about wilderness recreation, primarily in North America.

BACKPACKER magazine
33 East Minor Street
Emmaus, PA 18098
telephone 1-610-967-8181
web address: www.bpbasecamp.com

THE MOUNTAINEERS, founded in 1906, is a nonprofit outdoor activity and conservation club with 15,000 members, whose mission is "to explore, study, preserve, and enjoy the natural beauty of the outdoors. . . . " The club sponsors many classes and year-round outdoor activities in the Pacific Northwest, and supports environmental causes through educational activities, sponsoring legislation and presenting educational programs. The Mountaineers Books supports the club's mission by publishing travel and natural history guides, instructional texts, and works on conservation and history.

Send or call for our catalog of more than 300 outdoor titles:

The Mountaineers Books
1001 SW Klickitat Way, Suite 201
Seattle, WA 98134
1-800-553-4453
e-mail: mbooks@mountaineers.org
website: www.mountaineers.org

Other titles you may enjoy from The Mountaineers:

BACKPACKER'S EVERYDAY WISDOM: 1001 Expert Tips for Hikers,
Karen Berger
Tips and tricks for hikers and backpackers selected from the popular *BACKPACKER* magazine column, covering everything from packing and planning to field repairs and emergency improvisations.

BACKPACKER'S MAKING CAMP: A Complete Guide for Hikers, Mountain Bikers, Paddlers & Skiers,
Steve Howe, Alan Kesselheim, Dennis Coello, John Harlin
A comprehensive camping how-to compiled by *BACKPACKER* magazine field experts for anyone traveling by foot, boat, bicycle, or skis, through all kinds of terrain, year-round.

BACKPACKER'S BACKCOUNTRY COOKING: From Pack to Plate in Ten Minutes, *Dorcas S. Miller*
Over 140 easy, tasty recipes from a *BACKPACKER* magazine expert, including trail-tested tips from backcountry veterans. This cookbook offers advice on how to plan and pack simple and delicious meals.

WILDERNESS BASICS: The Complete Handbook for Hikers & Backpackers, *Jerry Schad & David S. Moser*
A handbook from the San Diego chapter of the Sierra Club, covering backcountry use from planning and equipment to weather and first aid.

A HIKER'S COMPANION: 12,000 Miles of Trail-Tested Wisdom,
Cindy Ross & Todd Gladfelter
An entertainingly written, real-life guide to surviving and thriving in the outdoors.

LIGHTLY ON THE LAND: The SCA Trail Building and Maintenance Manual, *Student Conservation Association*
The definitive, field-tested manual for anyone interested in wilderness trail building and maintenance.

JOHN MUIR: His Life and Letters and Other Writings, *Terry Gifford*
Rarely seen or published material gathered in one volume for the first time, including *Cruise of the Corwin; Picturesque California; Stickeen;* and more.

JOHN MUIR: The Eight Wilderness-Discovery Books, *John Muir*
The Story of My Boyhood and Youth; A Thousand Mile Walk to the Gulf; My First Summer in the Sierra; The Mountains of California; Our National Parks; The Yosemite; Travels in Alaska; Steep Trails.